THE LIFE AND TIMES OF GOGGA

CW01425676

NOEL G.

Strategic Book Publishing and Rights Co.

Strategic Book Publishing and Rights Co., LLC
USA | Singapore
www.sbpra.com

For information about special discounts for bulk purchases, please contact Strategic Book Publishing and Rights Co., LLC Special Sales, at bookorder@sbpra.net.

ISBN: 978-1-63135-939-2

To Bianca, my beautiful friend, colleague, and confidante, who has been by my side for more than fifteen years, through all my trials and tribulations. You have been superb; your help and friendship know no bounds, along with your lovely family. I am indebted to you now and always.

To my best mate, Stewart. What, as a family, would we have done without you? You have gone above and beyond the call of duty that any friendship deserves or demands. Words can never express the help, kindness, and time you have given to both my wife and me. We have a closeness that is unique, made with a friendship that's unending, and words can never express our thanks for this special bond.

To my pretend father-in-law, Andy. Your kindness and generosity, and that of your lovely wife, Linda, have been endless. To have you both as friends causes other friendships to pale nearly to insignificance. You're always there with your time and humour. You are, indeed, very special to me and your pretend daughter, and always will be.

To my beautiful wife, Meg, my soulmate and my best friend. I could wax lyrical about you and what you mean to me. You were and still are the love of my life. In the face of adversity, you have remained by my side, offering love and comfort, never putting yourself first. When we walk, we are as one: one couple, one shadow. I love you, sweetheart, and always will, forever and a day.

Not forgotten. To the people not mentioned but not forgotten, thank you for your kindness, prayers, and understanding through some really difficult times. Thank you for your friendship and care, and for always being there for us, as we will always be there for you.

CHAPTER 1

Gogga, the Beginning

Now, there's a name to conjure with. Born on December 22, 1948, at 23 Trafalgar Drive, Bebington, the second son in a dysfunctional family, I was made to suffer because no one ever spoke to me. Consequently, I made up my own words. Hence, the name Gogga (to be explained shortly).

The area where we lived was quite upmarket in as much as no one talked to each other. It was close to the beautiful village of Port Sunlight, which was unique. The village itself was built by Lord Leverhume for his factory workers. Can you see that happening today with these giant conglomerates? The factory produced soap products for nearly every country in the world, along with washing powders … practically everything that keeps you clean or makes you sparkle. Leaving the factory on a rainy day, you could arrive home covered in bubbles and spotlessly clean.

The village was beautiful, with incredible houses and its own church, school, art gallery, gardens, bank, bowling green, swimming baths, hotel, library, and shops. Hume Hall was one of the most beautiful buildings in the village, built for the people to hold their events, musical acts, and carnivals — a meeting place. The village also had its own post office and railway station bus service. It was so well thought out and was kept pristine. The gardens were amazing. There was also a boys club, where we held dances, etc.; a local football team, which I had the honour to play for; and, of course, our own pitch. I would imagine the village itself had won many awards and still does.

My father was a builder, a bricklayer, so when I was born, I had my very own crib … wait for it … made of bricks by his own fair hand — and lined, of course. Can you imagine it? It was like sleeping in a chimney. I can't say it was that comfortable, but they did their best. There again, what would I know about sleeping upright? There was no bird's nest, it appeared to be bombproof, and I didn't have any black-faced sweep sticking a brush up my arse to keep me clean.

No, my parents were a bit more adventurous than that when it came to washing, keeping clean, and saving water all at the same time. Kitchen sink. That was the kiddie. I went in with the dishes after tea. It was a good idea, as I had things to occupy my mind, like soapsuds, uneaten food, used teabags, knives, forks, small pans. … And I wasn't just put in. I was thrown in, mind you. In our sink, most things were. Then, when they became a health hazard or a danger to traffic, they got washed, along with me, and put back where they didn't belong.

There were always arguments about who would wash up after tea. It was usually the last man standing. They would shout and scream and throw things at each other: plates, knives, forks, me. The first four years of my life, I thought I was part of a circus act, there was so many things flying around. I could have had a job in the control tower at Heathrow Airport. It was educational. I learned to jump, duck, parry. You know, on reflection, I could have had a job in a circus as part of a trapeze act.

Gogga was a name I invented for my auntie, called Dolly Duckers (it gets better). I couldn't say Auntie Dolly. Gogga, for some reason, was the nearest I could get. She lived next door, and she raised my brother and me (Mum and Dad worked) in her own image, or nearly. Morons. Our kid was closest, because she talked to him. She was a little, fat woman. In fact, if she had been two inches shorter, she would have been perfectly round, and when she cuddled you, she could change the shape of your face.

But she had a heart of gold, and it's true to say we would have been lost without her—and sometimes we were, like when she would take us out shopping and forget to bring us home. Yes, she forgot we were with her and went home on her own. Can you imagine the impact that can have on a child? Here I was, sitting in the pram having a quick smoke (They all smoked in our family from an early age. I was nicknamed Kipper. I know now why.), thinking, *She has forgot me again.*

I was brought home by an agency called Find a Child (a bit like the RSPCA). It would be true to say I was a member. In fact, they were so bored with their jobs they used to take me home even when I wasn't lost. Strangers used to see me in the street and say, "I better take him home. Someone's forgotten him."

My Uncle Jack, Auntie Dolly's husband, I always thought was quite nasty. He had a wooden leg. Wooden legs seem to play a large part in my early life, as you will learn reading this magnificent piece of literature. He had a strange, livedin face, and I am convinced that when he was born, he tried to climb back in and got stuck.

Born in the streets of Bebington, just across the water from Liverpool and the mighty River Mersey ... you couldn't bathe in it, you couldn't swim in it, you couldn't paddle in it. Full of shit, pushchairs, shopping baskets, and salmon (still in its tin); the anglers used to go out fishing during the weekend to see what they could catch so they could have a week off work. There was nothing edible in the river. There was more life in a bag of crisps. I think the best you could hope for was maybe malaria; course, you would have to fall in to be really sure, and then some poor sod would have to come along and decontaminate you with something like petrol or Domestos. Ajax was popular. Three or four good, deep breaths could send you into orbit, which is where you'd need to be to fish the Mersey.

They say scientists in wartime used to do experiments in it, and they called the experiments scousers. Cheeky bastards. That's how we got our name; that and a pan stew someone threw together. Liverpool people are the salt of the earth. They're funny, and what's theirs is yours, unless they can get yours first, and without you knowing. It was a cliché in Liverpool, that things that come to those who wait are maybe the things of those who got there first. Think that out. I had to.

I was born three days before Christmas, on the 22nd of December at 11:50 p.m. at home. Dolly rushed in when she heard the screams of childbirth (she'd had five herself) and, with these welcoming words, "Christ, it's got a cock."

My mother only wanted girls, and the most frightening thing was that she had a poker in one hand and me in the other. She said she'd been about to poke the fire to keep me warm, but we will never know. My mum had a reputation for violence. On a scale from one to ten, she would score fifteen. It's possible this bestseller may never have been written and this author doomed because of her violence.

When childbirth came into play, my auntie used to go all God-fearing. As I say, she had five of her own, and when she was about to give birth, she would make her family join hands and follow her all round the house singing gospel songs, a bit like a religious hokey cokey. Now let's not forget this was the person who was going to bond with me — you know, Billy Graham meets the Simpsons (or in this case, the duckers).

So there I am, stuck between a religious lunatic and a three-wheeled pram (my brother needed the other wheel for his trolley). Every time I saw her, I went, "Gogga," and the name stuck. Everyone thought how clever it was of me to make up my own name for her, and here I am thinking I was trying to communicate with an alien. It maybe should have been "Ga-ga." Still, she did her best, and I am eternally grateful.

Like most builders, my dad liked a drink. He thought if he had enough, he could float home. Some nights, he did. My mother was a barmaid/cleaner/bottle-washer, you name it. She worked really hard, kept down three jobs at a time, so neither of them was ever in, but we were well cared for. Yes, we looked after ourselves.

My dad had a great sense of humour. I remember Dad coming home from work, sitting down in front of the TV, and a voice from the kitchen would sound, "What would you like for tea, darling? Chicken, beef, fish?"

"Thank you. Chicken, please," the reply came.

"You're having soup, you fat bastard. I was talking to the cat."

People would not see that as funny, but it was, and it's the way they were with each other, except when they were fighting and my mum was beating my dad up. I remember one night when he had floated home, she smashed a red-hot pot of tea on his head. My dad was sitting there with third-degree burns all over his head and my mum complaining that the teapot was a family heirloom, and irreplaceable. You know, my dad never raised his hands, never hit my mum. I think, on reflection, that just made her worse.

Latchkey kids. We could do anything, and we did. We could wash, iron, cook, clean, steal. We knew more about looking after a house than our parents will ever know.

We lived in a semi with an outside toilet, which was right next to the coal shed. When you went for a shit and pulled the chain, you got covered in coal dust, so if you had the runs, you could walk round all day like one of the black-and-white minstrels. The secret was newspaper Toilet rolls wasn't the thing the thing then, it was a six inch nail with old newspapers cut into squares attached to the nail, It had two applications: One was for wiping your bum (not the nail) and the other was so you could make a paper hat to keep the dust off. Didn't always work, but you didn't cough as much.

Bathtime. Well, that was about to change forever. You see, in those days, everyone bathed in an old tin bath shaped like a Zulu's boat, placed in front of the fire to keep you warm. The bath was flat, so the older you got, the deeper you went. This was done quite technically by placing a brick under one end of the bath, thus raising it slightly and pushing the water down to create a deep end. The older you got, the deeper you went.

There was always a pecking order: Mum, Dad, the dog, Granddad, and me. Believe me, when it was my turn, the gravy was so thick on the top you needed the help of a shovel to get in. It was like bathing in pea soup, and the colour was similar as well.

As I say, things were about to take a miraculous turn. The envy of the street. My dad, in one of his sober moments, thought a proper bath was needed and decided it could go in the spare room upstairs, and so we had the first indoor bath in the street. When it was installed, the whole street knew about it, as it was sticking out the front of the house. (My father never measured anything.) Not all of it, course — just up to the taps. But we were the first ones. The pecking order didn't change, but you had privacy and a warm place for the shovel (the gravy was just as thick, and the colour never changed).

I started school (Stanton Road) when I was four years old. You were supposed to start at five, but my mother lied, and I have no idea why. I think it was because dropping me off at Grandma's was getting to be too much and my auntie's memory wasn't what it was. She was still leaving me places but couldn't remember where. The walk to Grandma's was about half an hour, and all uphill. When we got there, we travelled over cobblestones to the front door, so I was like a milkshake by the time they got me out of the pram. There was always a strange smell in the house, an old smell. I just put that down to my granddad. He was pleased, in a way, to see me. He used to pick me up, sit me on his knee, fart, and then put me down again. It was like a ritual.

School, my first day, could have been better. I somehow got in trouble the first day for, of all things, fighting. I could not understand why all the kids were in short trousers and this one boy was in long ones. It took just two minutes to find out. I told him to drop his trousers. As a young fashion icon and a nosey little sod, I could see myself in them. He clipped me around the ear, so I kicked him in the shin. Shit, did that hurt!

Those pants were hiding a wooden leg. The teacher demanded I apologise — me, the injured party. I told her to get a life. What about my injured toe?

To which she responded, "I have a life, but yours will be very short if you don't say sorry."

So I did. The bastard just laughed, so I spent the next six years planning revenge, all sorts of things. The best one was gluing his leg to the floor (just under the foot) while he still had it on and was asleep, and he could doze off at a moment's notice. I got the blame for that, which seemed reasonable, as I had done it.

Anyway, back to my first day at school. The teachers decided it was a good idea to let me play in the sandpit. Whose idea it was to bury me in there, I will never know, but this I can say: the bastards were lucky I never found out. I had sand everywhere, you can bet your life. By going-home time, the teachers wished they had ordered the cement to go with it.

It was quite strange at primary school. Everything was a challenge. Not more so than finding my way there. My mother, in her wisdom, every school morning sent me to school with jam on toast sandwiches for my breakfast. By the time I arrived, I had eaten them, which was just as well, as it was nearly lunchtime when I got there. The teachers couldn't understand why it took me so long to get to school, but I didn't even have a map. Talk about understanding things; they were quite baffled at me constantly turning up in the summer holidays when we were off. I just put it down to communication difficulties between my parents and the school.

Today, of course, social services would probably get involved and say I had been abandoned, and they wouldn't be far wrong. They couldn't understand why I had no friends during the summer holidays. They didn't realise there was no bugger there to play with when I arrived.

Roy Orbison, I am sure, heard about my misadventures and wrote a song about me called "Only the Lonely." I should have realised climbing over the gates instead of walking through them was a problem, but as a five-year-old, you don't. I mean, as most young kids, I enjoyed my own company, which was just as well, I suppose, as there was only me to enjoy.

Back to my adversary, the hated one-legged monster. The next chance I had to wreak revenge arrived when he fell asleep after lunch one day, and he did sleep a lot. That bloody thing (the wooden leg) just wouldn't burn, but I managed to singe the braces holding it up and burn a hole in his trousers. After being accused, I was sent to the headmistress (that should read "headcase"). Her name was Miss Montgomery, and she told me how naughty I was and caned me. She gave me a letter for my mother, saying this had to stop. She then gave me a sweet. I would like to think that the sweet was for my ingenuity in finding a way to glue the bugger's leg to the floor, and the caning was for getting caught.

The strangest thing that happened to me was when I caught my form teacher in the toilets with another teacher. She said she was adjusting his tie. I thought it quite odd as his trousers were round his ankles. I thought, *Tie? Shit, it must go all the way down to his socks.* As a child, you would think that. As an adult, you would think, *Lucky bastard.* He had a sort of elastic keeping his socks up, which seemed to enlarge his knees, and they appeared to stick together, probably to shorten his tie (as the teacher would like us to believe), or to stop his balls from dropping too far, as was probably the case.

The male teacher she was with was a good teacher. He had no favourites; he hated everyone. He would come in Monday morning

(Sunday must have been a horrible day for him). It was his revenge day for a shitty weekend.

Most normal people would work out their aggression in the gym or on a long walk, or even kick the dog. Not him. He had a class full of fresh kids. While he was dishing out his punishment, he kept the best till last, and usually for me. They called it Angela.

Now, Angela in herself was a nice girl, but she had one problem: a very weak bladder. She had obviously never heard of the toilet or been pottytrained. Sitting beside Angela was, in itself, a challenge. She was so nervous sitting by boys that her bladder went to pieces. She could piss all over you twenty times a day. The desks we sat at were like forms. As I was slightly heavier than Angela, there was a slight leaning to my end, so every time she pissed, you could see a trail of water attacking me. The challenge was, of course, to get pissed on only ten times a day. She got so excited sitting by anyone male that she just couldn't help herself. As I say, her bladder just went to pieces, and over the poor bastard that had to sit beside her.

This was the teacher's idea of punishment — quite sick, really, and you were if she got too close. I remember her trying to kiss me once. She reached over, farted, and I got the blame for that as well. The teacher said I was disgusting and made me stand outside the classroom which, in itself, was a bit of a relief, really. It gave me chance to take stock, get dry, and piss off home.

This was, of course, another problem I had. The teachers tried to explain to me that I had to arrive and go home at schooltime with the rest of the kids, not my time. We obviously couldn't agree, so I resigned, I thought. But no. My parents tried to come to some sort of deal with me by promising not to send me during weekends.

I can remember one Monday morning when Angela was in spar-kling form. She never stopped pissing and farting all day. The teacher held a question-and-answer session of what we would all like to be, and when he asked me, the only answer I could think of was "dry." I was the only kid who used to come to school on a

Monday in rubber trousers. (You guessed it. Angela and I were bonding, hence the rubber trousers.) At the end of the day, you went home damp, very damp. I used to have those wrinkles and webbed fingers that you get when you spend too long in the bath, and I smelled like a sumo wrestler's jockstrap. Even my fingers were starting to stick together. If Angela's parents had any concern for their daughter and the poor bastards that had to sit by her, you would think they would have invested in a rubber suit or a catheter. The only way she could keep dry was by sitting in one of those sand buckets. At the end of the school day, she would walk home like John Wayne, her poor legs chapped to hell. I couldn't wait for the weekend to come, even if it was only to see water that was a different colour.

My weekend consisted of generally getting into trouble, which I had a gift for, but really, I was just a normal kid trying to find a way of having some fun usually at other peoples expense. I always got caught. I had this thing of wanting my enemies to know it was me (they had a bloody good idea anyway). For one so small and so young, I was always up for a challenge and a good hiding when they caught me. Shit, I was grounded more often than the Concorde.

I can remember we had one game, it was called knick knock, where you knocked on someone's door and then ran away. We had one lad — and trust me, there's always one — called David. This silly sod got right into the game to such a state that when it was time to go home, his brain was somewhere else. I remember him knocking on his own door and running away. Don't forget: We had finished, gone home. God knows how he got in.

When we went scrumping (borrowing apples without the owner's permission), we used to pinch them from a guy who lived near the railway station. They called him Nelson because he only had one eye, and the bugger must have been in the middle of his head. He always had this canny knack of knowing when we where around. Nothing to do with his apple trees being emptied, of course. Christ, was he quick, like shit off a shovel. Now, he would kick your arse if he got hold of you — always chased you in slippers, owing to the strange nature of his feet. They were like wooden clogs. Can you imagine wearing slippers over them? It was like being chased by a human skateboard, only without the wheels. He would have been brilliant on snow, the Jean Claude Killey of Bromborough Road. It was a relief to see them flying over your head. You knew then he was slowing down out of breath.

My other highlight of the weekend was going to see my grandma for Sunday lunch. They lived down a cobblestone lane in a two-up two-down terraced house with gas mantles for lighting. It was like something out of Charles Dickens, and that was only the way they dressed. When you walked through the door, you could smell the beef cooking like only your grandma can cook it. She used to give us thick slices of bread to dip into the hot beef dripping. It was heaven. You don't hear or see anything like that anymore. Some things you never forget; even today, that is a big miss. Just writing about the beef cooking and the dripping sizzling, I can smell it. As we walked through the door, she would give you a thick slice of bread to dip into the hot dripping, but even when cold, spread on toast, it was just heaven.

Before starting lunch, we always had to wait for my granddad, a colourful old character (should read nasty), to come home from a pub called The George. This was just down the road from where they lived. Granddad would arrive, usually black and blue, always on a stretcher. My granddad loved fighting. He had more fights than Popeye; never won any. They christened him the Horizontal Champion of Bebington. Whomever he picked on used to give him a good hiding, and my dad and my Uncle Stan used to rush down to the pub with the stretcher to collect him. He was brought home like the pope, only lying down.

Once they brought him round from his drunken stupor and beating, they would take him upstairs to bed, and one weekend he came through the ceiling. Those old houses must have been built by some tribe out of Africa. They echoed, were cold, and the lighting was gas mantles. We had a cast-iron fireplace with ovens on either side, and in all honesty, it was probably worth more than the house.

Back to Granddad and his dilemma. You could see his little legs dangling, plaster falling all over the dinner table, and the noise! He nearly died. He was screaming for help, but nobody was allowed to leave the table till lunch was finished, and Grandma told him not to shout so loud, as it was Sunday.

All she could say on looking up was, "He's ripped his trousers and he hasn't changed his socks, dirty sod."

It didn't matter that the poor bugger's vital organs were stuck under his chin or the blood dripping on the tablecloth was his. She just moved the table and we all ate lunch. After about ten minutes, it all went quiet.

She said, "The drunken sod's fallen asleep."

As it happened, the poor bugger was unconscious and in a coma. They ran for an ambulance — well, ambled actually, as everyone there refused to give him the kiss of life, which gives you an idea of how highly rated he was in the popularity stakes. He and Sadsam Hussein were neck and neck as to whom you would prefer to have lunch. When Granddad started, he would sit at the table, fart, snort, grunt, and he was still hesitant to pick up his knife and fork. You could have been eating out at Chester Zoo, so Saddam would win by a whisker.

Waiting for the ambulance to arrive, he was lying there in what must have been agony. You had to feel sorry for the poor old bugger, but all you could hear was Grandma shouting, "Does anyone want any apple pie and custard?"

Life then was so up in the air. People looked after each other because all they had was each other. How times change. People's doors were open to almost anyone, and your goods were safe. That would never happen today. The bastards would not only take your goods, they would take the doors as well and then try and sell them back to you.

I loved my grandma. Though I was young, I do remember her and believe she looks over me today, and that gives me a sense of belonging, which helps in the strange times we live in. I often talk to her, and I know she listens. It's quite incredible and hard to believe my granddad bought her for a bottle of gin and ten shillings in old money, fifty pence today. What a bargain. He took her back to his hovel in a horse and trap with a mattress on board. She used to take in washing and ironing to supplement their income, and he would come home from the pub and throw everything on the floor and stamp all over it for her to start over again. How nasty was that!

She was only a frail woman, but made up for it in many ways. I found out of late that he was superstitious. My grandma used to read cups, tea leaves, palms. She had an amazing gift, which was passed down to my mum. He obviously thought or had some weird idea that it would be lucky to have someone of Grandma's ilk in his household.

It's hard to comprehend how life has changed, for the worse, I believe, in some cases. There appears to be very little compassion in the world. Its dog-eat-dog attitudes have changed today. Love thy neighbour doesn't happen; it's been replaced by what's yours is mine and what's mine is my own.

Grandma's house itself had a bit of history. It was owned previously by my great-granddad, who kept a chimpanzee. He had this animal when he was in the navy, and when he later gave up the sea, it became his companion. One night when he came home drunk, he forgot to light the gas mantle and the chimpanzee panicked, attacked him, and bit his throat out. Now, this animal had been with him for eight years. The vet said the animal panicked in the dark, believing it was in danger. That was the only animal fatality we had in the family apart from when Granddad ate the next door neighbour's dog, but that's another story for another time.

I suppose, in general, Granddad was enjoying being a miserable old sod. He never had much time for anybody except himself. I can remember him coming home one Sunday at lunchtime drunk as a lord. He always fell asleep in his chair, as did all the grownups after lunch, which was a great time for me to create some mischief. You know, bored, idle hands and all that. My favourite trick was to stick dried peas up Granddad's nose, point him at the cat, and wait for him to sneeze. You could never be sure where they would go, but shit! The speed they would fly out of his nostrils was incredible, accompanied by a long line of snot, a bit like Haley's Comet with attitude, and other bits and pieces. He would sneeze so much his eyeballs nearly popped out of his head. He was just covered in a cobweb of snot (as was the cat) that seemed to go hard on contact, and the poor cat stood there like someone had thrown a net over it, looking a little bit shabby, like somebody had rescued it from the toilet and, may I say, very pissed off.

I remember them once discussing when he fell off the settee in a drunken stupor. As he lay there overnight, cockroaches crawled into his mouth, where they laid eggs. In those days, beer was very sweet and attracted almost everything you can think of. But let me tell you, if they had seen him in daylight and covered in snot the week before, there's no way the little buggers would have bothered. The doctor had to feed him poison to kill off the eggs. Grandma always said the doctor didn't give him enough and that the cockroaches had already been punished by crawling into his mouth.

The other thing I remember quite vividly was that they had an outside toilet with newspaper attached to a nail to wipe your bum on (not the nail — the paper). It was cold and damp (the toilet and the paper), and though you were desperate for a pee, you just couldn't. It just wasn't possible. The toilet bowls in them days were so high off the floor and deep that you needed a ladder and a lifeguard to go for a shit. If you fell in, you could be missing for a week and never be found; either that or you would surface in your neighbour's toilet, which was another serious problem that came to light.

You were always told to pull the chain and open the door. Not a lot has changed today. They tell you to pull the chain and open the window. I remember being blamed for not pulling the chain, which is something I have always done. Anyway, I was sent out to see what I was supposed to have left in the bog. Well, you could have knocked me down with a feather. There was the biggest turd I had ever seen; this was not left by a human. I'm saying that I am quite sure it had a pulse. It had certainly never shaved — it was like a hairy sock. Well, I couldn't pass that in a month of Sundays, never mind out of my arse. It was like something you find begging in the street. Whoever it was didn't need a doctor's help; he needed Dyno-Rod.

I had strict instructions to get rid of it. Well, I fought with it for about an hour. They gave me a dust pan, shovel, and a brush to get it out, but they might as well have given me a lead to take it for a fucking walk. The only thing it didn't have was eyebrows and teeth. Arnold Schwarzenegger would have been proud to act with that in the film *The Turdanator*. Ha ha, joke. I had come to the conclusion someone had grown it and shoved it down the bog as a joke. I mean, when I got it out, it was nearly as tall as me. How could they possibly think it was mine?

There was something else quite strange about Granddad. Grandma had two cats, and it's true about animals having a sixth sense. As soon as they left the room, my granddad used to let out the most horrendous fart, and they say you could smell it down at the pub. What's more, he had been known to follow through, if you know what I mean. Hell, you would need a bomb disposal squad just to relieve him of his trousers and empty them somewhere safe, like the local dump (ha! There's a pun: "dump").

Back to my bog duties. I can honestly say I fought with that turd for about a week. Well, I didn't. It just felt like a week, but the good thing was that its brother (I assumed there could be a family of them) appeared in the middle of the week while I was at school, so it couldn't have been me. Imagine, though. A family of turds like that.

It turned out it was the woman next door called Eric, which was a strange name for a woman, I know. When these things kept dropping out of her arse, her toilet quite naturally was getting blocked, so in her infinite wisdom, she was using Grandma's. I wouldn't mind. She lived right next to a farmer's field. She could have walked it in two minutes, took them with her, and left them there, where the flies could picket them as a disaster area. Don't land here. Unsafe. This is a turd-free zone.

When my grandma died — well, just before she did — she told me I wouldn't see her anymore, but not to worry because she had been to a beautiful place called Heaven, with flowers, rolling fields of green, corn. You could get sunburnt off its beauty. She said to never be afraid of death, that the only thing to fear in life is fear itself. She was quite ill. The doctor had given her tablets that didn't seem to be working, and within the hour, she died. They found a load of tablets under her tongue. She had never swallowed them. She had just given up; the thought of being saved must have been purgatory to her. I guess she'd just had enough, and seeing what she had seen in God's garden was the ultimate, a no-brainer.

CHAPTER 2

Getting There

When Grandma died, Granddad came to live with us, which, in a way, wasn't too bad. It gave me someone else to experiment on. He was out to make everyone's life a misery, so he was fair game. His room stank of all sorts of things, from stale cigarettes to farts and burps. Someone needed to paint a big red cross on the door and let people know they were entering the twilight zone.

It was my job to wake him up in the morning with some tea. I poured the tea into his boot before entering my grandfather's bedroom, as I thought he would be asleep. He would then throw one of his hobnail boots at me always the one with the tea in it to let me know he was awake. I only ever heard him laugh once; that was when my mum was beating me up. What a sad old bastard.

It was quite a strange relationship my grandparents had. I know I have already said this once, but again, he bought my grandma for ten shillings and half a bottle of gin. Ten shillings in today's money is fifty pence. You couldn't buy a goldfish in a bag for that. You can't visualise that in today's world, or I can't, anyway. As I have said, it must have been like winning the jackpot for him and purgatory for her.

She used to take in washing and ironing to make ends meet. He used to take in as much drink as possible, and when he came home and saw the washing hanging out, he was known to pull it off the line and stamp all over it. What on earth would annoy you enough to want to do that? It beggars belief. He didn't deserve my grandma, so he really was fair game. His other problem was he had this horse and trap, and the horse was constantly drunk he used to feed it buckets of beer if that horse its name escapes me for the moment hadn't had four legs it would never have got home.

We were brought up to believe in the spirit world. Our family dates back to the Viking invasion. We were half-Viking, half-Romany gypsy. We are also mentioned in the Domesday Book, which seems about right for some reason. I think our family, though I have never checked, has a fair bit of history about it. Back in those days of old, everyone had a Christian name or first name. Their surname was usually associated with the village they were born in and was carried through the generations.

My mother and grandmother used to read tea leaves and cards. The day my grandma died, as I have already mentioned, I was there, and she said she had just visited Heaven and it was a beautiful place. She said we must never fear death. It doesn't exist; only ever-lasting life is real, and now it was time for her to go, and she died. Goodnight and God bless, Grandma. Thank you for being you and for looking over me.

Monday morning soon came around. Back to school, back to Angela, back to that bastard with a wooden leg. Trying to stay out of the toilets in case Hansel and Gretel were in there straightening each other's tie. If there was one thing I hated about school, it was those bloody toilets. To sit on them, you had to have an arse like two eggs in a hanky, and as for going for a shit, well, was that tricky or what? You needed to be a bloody magician. As for the toilet paper they supplied, there was just nothing like it: greasy on both sides (I think it was called Izal). It was pure bloody torture. It had to have been invented by the Japanese. Who on earth in their right mind thought it up? They definitely never used it. Once you started to wipe your arse, your fingers started skiing everywhere. You never knew where it would finish up. One thing's for sure — it wasn't down the pan. Trousers, socks, legs, underpants, the back of your shoes, but not the pan.

Christmastime was coming round, and I was just waiting to see if Santa Claus had committed suicide again, or been arrested for being drunk in charge of a sleigh. I can remember being at my uncle's for one Christmas and waking up. I say waking up — I was sleepwalking and walked into the wrong room, only to find my auntie with her legs wrapped around Santa Claus's waist. She told me if I didn't go back to sleep, Santa wouldn't come, but little did she know, he already had … all over my fucking sheets and half my presents.

Back at school, I was going to be in my first play: a star. I was to play Joseph in the Nativity, I thought, but as more and more people came to the rehearsals (I was originally the only one to turn up), my role was severely diminished. It became different: First, one of the kings, then the innkeeper, then one of the shepherds, and the producer finally decided I would be a good milkman. Please remember this is the Nativity, only two thousand years ago (nothing to do with associated dairies). I could have had the role as the goat, but I only had two legs, so I ended up the goat's butler — another bloody insult. Talking about insults, Trixie someone got the part of Mary, and she had spots on her face you could hide behind. You would swear she'd been growing oranges and some bugger tried to peel them. On a dark night, she could frighten a ghost, but somehow she got a starring role.

That wasn't fair. She was a good friend. I remember trying to get my hands in her pants on many occasions, and I didn't know whether it was lust or love till Miss Seed came along, and she changed my hormones for life. That comes a little later.

Stardom? Not this year. The only words I had to speak were: "Two pints." Think about it. Two sodden pints. Who ordered pints two thousand years ago? What a letdown. Even Ugly Moore had a better part. We called Ugly Moore that because he was. Come to think of it, even his parents called him that. He had a strange expression, like someone had sat on his face when it was warm. He used to go to counselling sessions because of his looks, poor bastard. He wasn't a pretty sight. His psychiatrist would only see him if he laid facedown on the couch. Yes, to my utter amazement, even he had a prime part as one of the kings.

Anyway, back to my lines. "Two pints." Please! My father would have been proud of me, and Heaven forbid, I nearly blew that. There on opening night, sitting in the audience in the front row, was the water-carrier, Angela. Now, that was quite off putting. Strange, because we could have used her that evening, as some silly sod (not me) tried to burn the stage down. Another unsatisfied star, Brian the Arsonist (at least that's what the police called him), was to blame, but all fingers pointed at me being the nearest when the fire started. Then they thought it was a stray fag someone had left behind, which, may I add, was a good year before I started smoking, so at least I was in the clear. In those days, you could buy loose cigarettes. You could buy them in ones and twos, with matches attached.

Anyway, back to the play. In a word, I flopped in the play. How could you do that with only two words to say? It's not like you need a prompter, is it? I can only think I was underwhelmed by the occasion. It was about this time I failed my audition for the choir as well. Again, it was only me who turned up. If that's not a choker, what is? He asked me what I wanted to sing, and I said, "What about Bill Haley's 'Rock Around the Clock'?" He said, "No, you've missed the point."

Back to Angela. My confidence was shattered. I was disillusioned. She sat for a good hour and never once pissed on anyone. How cruel can the world be! And to top it all, that smug twat with the wooden leg got a leading part in the play and, as he was at the far end of the stage with this stupid grin on his face, I just couldn't get to him or do any damage.

My next exciting moment came when we had a fancy dress party at school, so I asked my mum what I should go as. Neither of us had a clue, and as my mum was always at work, she didn't have a lot of time to help. She kept asking what I thought, but I just didn't have any idea. At last, all my constant moaning gave her the idea she needed. She put a floppy hat on my head, put me in pyjamas with tape round my mouth and a candle in my hand, gave me a big drum, and sent me as "Silent Night," which, under pressure, was pretty good. I didn't win anything, but you have to admit, what an imagination!

The following year, bearing in mind she had a year to think about this, she nearly got me killed. She sent me dressed as a sweet shop, with chocolates and candy and other various sweets hanging from me. I didn't even get in the auditorium. I was mugged by about thirty kids and left in a pile of sweets' papers and wrappings. What on earth was she thinking? I knew there was going to be trouble. On my way there, I was followed by a dozen dogs, all with their tongues hanging out, sniffing chocolate. I felt like the Pied Piper of Stanton Road, so we agreed no more fancy dress.

I am now eight, a man of the world — in my mind, grownup. For the first time, I am in love. I have moved up a class and my teacher is Miss Seed. She was wonderful. My first coming of age, and my first erection. She looked nice, she smelt nice, and the first glimpse of her knickers just sent me into orbit. She used to get me to stand next to her and read to the class, with her arm around me and my penis going up and down like a bell rope. I had my first stutter.

I was probably the best reader we had. Some would say the only reader we had. We certainly were not a bright bunch. In fact, if you painted us all orange, we wouldn't stand out in a crowd. Everyone was focused on playtime and morning break, where we had our breakfast and milk, then lunchtime and a game of cards and a smoke. The dinners were absolute shit. They always had a thing called cabbage with potatoes—which, may I add, Sir Walter Raleigh certainly didn't bring back from America—and something we were always told was good for us (semolina), but no one outside the kitchen staff and testing laboratories could explain just what it was. It tasted like cardboard or the pages of an old book, and when they put jam on it, it looked like a monk's breast. Not that I know, you understand, but a monk's breast probably tasted a hell of a lot better.

It's my thinking that these primary schools used us kids as guinea pigs for the third-world countries. If we would eat it, so would they. So, to continue the meaning of our day, after lunch, looking forward to playtime, staying as far away from Angela as possible for obvious reasons, and then going-home time three o'clock. We might have been tired during the day, but come three o'clock, we came out of that school like we had been shot out of a bloody cannon. We headed to the nearest field, football boots on, and about four or five of us kicking a ball about. That lasted about an hour, till we were hungry, then we were off home.

My first job upon getting home was taking the dog for a walk. Poor bugger, it was the only dog on the street with an identity crisis. Everyone at home had a different name for it, and sometimes when I was out and somebody called out a name, the dog would stop and look at me as if to say, "Do I answer that?" It was really confused. It had more names than the Secret Service. We had a succession of dogs, and they all had an affliction of one type or another. In saying that, I had two goldfish I won at the fairground. I told the fairground worker I didn't want them, so he threatened to do me serious harm if I didn't take them. It was obvious he didn't want them either. I found out you have to be very careful with goldfish. You can only feed them once a day. Well, after two weeks, these buggers had turned green. We could not figure out why. Needless to say, they were dead. We didn't know if it was lack of food, people using the bowl as an ashtray, or the pound of fag ash in the bottom of the bowl that killed them. Even smoker's cough wasn't ruled out.

Those poor animals must have wondered what they had let themselves in for. My mum brought home an Alsatian and she wanted to call it Woozy or Tootsie. I ask you, an Alsatian called Woozy or Tootsie is just like calling Mike Tyson "Mary." You don't, do you? Apparently it was just a cat she wanted, but when she found the dog tied up outside somebody's house, she said it looked unwanted. Can you imagine the identity crisis that dog would have suffered? It would have thrown itself under the nearest bus. Thankfully, the owner who had left it tied up managed to rescue it.

We only had a small backyard, so pet-wise, I had to be careful of what I kept in such a small space. I had this chicken with a limp called Norman, and I built its cage next to the coal shed. It used to walk around all day covered in coal dust and sneezing. Now, that bird really did need counselling. It would lay eggs, then bury them. I ask you, what sort of chicken does that? When we got it, we thought, "Great, fresh eggs!" But finding them was something else. It used to crow at the crack of dawn — you know, about ten thirty. Lazy bastard. When I got it, I was told it was an old bird, quite experienced. An old bird? More like a bloody granny. It needed a fucking walking stick. I will always remember the day it died and what we had for tea. My dad said it had committed suicide — you know, threw itself under an axe. I was really upset and wouldn't eat it, so he got me another one. I called this one Henry, remembering the axe.

CHAPTER 3

Long Days

The days were quite long in school, young and innocent. And when they tried to teach you something, they were even longer. I liked the winter days, myself, with long lie-ins if it was too cold to go to school. Some friends and I used to sneak off down an entry at the back of some houses close to where I lived. There was an old Ford parked there, had been for years, so we used to hide in that till all the parents went to work, then sneak (or break) into a house closeby, make ourselves hot chocolate, and go to bed. We'd wake up at noon and go home for lunch. We had it made. They had an electric meter that they put coins in to pay for the electricity they used, so we would empty that, and in the afternoons, we would go to the pictures. What a life! The mischief we got up to was bizarre. We used to run onto the golf course, pinch the balls as they landed … well, our dog did … and sell them back to the golfers. We had imagination. We used to organise our own Olympics and World Cup.

Today, the kids struggle to get dressed. You have to wonder how some of them found their way out of the birth canal. We had no TV, you see — just each other, and imagination.

I had a mentor. Well, actually, he was a criminal mentor … well, petty criminal, that is. I didn't know that at the time. I used to help in the summer bag coal with him. At night, so that should give you a clue. It certainly was for the coal board. That was the best thing, working with Bill. You were always sure of a bit of pocket money, and always a warm thanks to the coal board. He used to get me to climb over walls at the hospices and old people's homes, stealing the blankets off them as they lie on stretchers outside the buildings and inside the hallways. He always told me they were dead, and most of them were, I say. Most of them. I remember taking the blanket off one and it turned over. I thought, *Shit! There is no way that's dead,* and I ran for my life (that's no joke). We would then sell the blankets to the rag-and-bone merchants.

He always said there's good money in rags; then there was the day he asked me to strip the lead off this bungalow. I said, "Is that legal, climbing the drainpipe?"

He said, "Yes, no problem. I forgot the ladders." He told me the local council had been in touch and was short of lead.

I said, "Does anyone live there?"

He said, "No, not really."

I said, "There is smoke coming out of the chimney."

He said, "I lit a fire to warm the roof." (The things you believe when you're a kid.) The next thing, as I am taking the slates off and throwing the lead down, this little old dear appears, shouts up, "Excuse me, would you like a cup of tea?"

I thought, *House empty, my arse.* All you could hear was Bill taking off down the street on his bike. Well, everyone could hear him, as the bike had no tyres on it.

He was a good soul, but the day came when I thought, *Enough is enough.* We were passing the coal yard when he spots a hundredweight brick on the road. They used them for weighing off sacks of coal. He said, "I will drive past slowly," (he had this crappy van) "and you open the door and pick it up. When you've grabbed it and it's in your hand, tell me and I will drive off."

So he passes it slowly, I grab hold of it, tell him I've got it, and he drives off. The weight stayed on the road, with my hand wrapped around it. It pulled my torso out of the van onto the road. There I am, flat-out kissing the tarmac. Bear in mind, there is not a lot of me. It was just too heavy, and I didn't have the brains or the speed to let go. By this time, Bill has gone (He was a good mate like that. If he thought there may be trouble, he would just leave you.), and here I am, hugging the tarmac, smelling the fumes of that poxy old van tearing off up the road.

Summer arrived at last. The summer days then seemed a lot warmer than today's, and there seemed to be more of them. Maybe there is something about this global warming. There we were, a group of us boys and girls, but every day we did something different to amuse ourselves — different games. We created fishing, camping. There were no computers, no electronic games. The kids today would be lost if these things didn't exist. We all used to congregate round the old railway works.

I can remember the day the whole gang got together and we turned over a railway carriage. Sod's law, we get caught by the local police. The noise of the carriage hitting the ground must have woken them up. Shit, were we in trouble then! I mean, we were in and out of police stations for general misdemeanours and the odd court appearance, but nothing serious — just a slap on the wrist or probation or that sort of thing. Well, this was totally different. This could mean a jail sentence, we thought.

Being in court a few times, the worst thing that can happen to you is when the judge or the magistrate calls you by your first name. He asked was anyone there to speak for me. Looking around, the only three words I could think of were "in the shit." My brother was there and spoke on my behalf and for the family. He asked where my parents were. Well, it was Grand National Day, so my mum was in the bookies and my dad was doing his social thing, visiting the local pubs. So my brother, in his wisdom and thinking about my pocket money that could be his, said, "I apologise. Noel's parents couldn't be here. Could the court hang on to the boy for a few months, as he has become unstable and I believe a fresh environment would be good for him."

Of course, the judge agreed, sentencing me to six months in borstal. This was going to change my life forever (or could have if the strange guards and sorry teachers had gotten their way). I was thirteen and a half years old. You had to think on your feet, and I was quite switched-on, taking into account the environment I was brought up in. In these places, you learn quick: Never be caught alone, do as you are told. You were slapped from pillar to post either by the teachers (they thought it was nicer than calling them wardens) or other inmates till you hit back, which only landed you in more trouble, but you had to, even though you ended up worse for wear. When they hit you, they were cute. No marks, like those left by truncheons. They didn't have to hit you hard; once or twice in the same place was enough. On my release (I say release. I was coming up to fourteen, so they transferred me to a different unit.), I think they just wanted to know if I was still going to be a menace. Believe me, I wasn't. The transfer was good for me: more schooling, less hard labour.

There were some sad cases in there. Some were beaten, and some liked to be beaten. In a sad way, they viewed it as affection. Some arrived for doing very little — pinching fruit, etc. — but they knew upon entering those gates that they would be warm and fed, and when you're cold and hungry, maybe a beating doesn't seem too bad. There was a bit of camaraderie; you could hear muffled cries at night. We were all in a dormitory, each dorm had ten beds, and there were three dorms, so nothing was private. If they were not crying, farting, or snoring, they were playing with themselves. Some even cuddled each other. One used to suck his thumb and sleep in the foetal position.

Breakfast was at eight thirty every morning, and you had to eat it all. This was after a long run, every morning except Sunday, then back to the dorm. There, we showered and had breakfast, which you ate or you were forcefed; the food was, in all fairness, shit.

Lunch at twelve o'clock, dinner at five o'clock, a cup of hot chocolate at eight thirty in the evening. There was spare time when we
were not in school; this came after lunch till four thirty and was
usually taken up by gardening duties outside — moving a hole
from one end of the garden to the other — or in the greenhouse
with tomatoes and other produce.

The place was spotless but in the schoolroom; the desks looked
like they had been run over by a tractor. They had a boxing gym; I
say a boxing gym. They taught you self-defence, which was just
another excuse for them to beat you up.

I didn't enjoy it, and at times it was quite frightening, especially
if some idiot went berserk, and that happened a few times. One
no-brainer tried to throw himself through a window; pointless, as
it had bars on the other side. He ended up on the escape committee, of which he was the only one. They used to call him Stalag
John, he was so desperate to get out. I suppose it was akin to being
stir-crazy. Some kids just lost it, and were punished for it. There was
no sympathy shown to anyone or by anyone. It was a very strict
regime; you couldn't show a weakness.

Every dormitory had a bully, usually a lot older than the kids in
that dorm. This guy was called Ralph, and I always said (not to his
face, of course) that if I ever met him in the street, he wouldn't bully
anybody else. He tried it on me. He said, "What sort of name is
gobshite? Why don't you get any visitors?"

I said, "My brother has just been released from Walton jail. He
should be here today or tomorrow."

"Really?" he said in a snide manner. "Which old lady did he
rob?"

I said, "He didn't. He shot one guy and put the other one in a
wheelchair. I will introduce you when he arrives."

"Why would you want to do that?"

I said, "He may have some encouraging words for you."

"Is that a threat?" was his reply.

I said, "We can ask him tomorrow, or on his next visit."

My brother never did anything like that, but it kept that piece of shit away from me. It didn't stop me filling a sock with pebbles and taping it to the inside leg of my pants. I was expecting something, and that would be the only protection I would have. I was convinced I would only get one chance if he jumped me, but nothing happened. Whether it was because someone told him what I had in mind and what was in store for him or he was what I thought, just a bully, I don't know.

Time dragged and people were starting to get on everyone's nerves, but my time was nearly over. I didn't make any friends, but you couldn't risk being on your own. It was that fear that made you stick together, a fear that made you strong, a fear I hope never comes into my life again.

Release date came with no one there to meet and greet. I got the bus, went as far as three pence would take me, and walked the rest. The family was surprised to see me, as they were not told what was happening. At first, they asked if I had run away. I said no. I had a piece of paper with a stamp on it saying "Released."

I didn't want to go back there. I didn't learn much, except that there are a lot of kids a hell of a lot worse than me who, in hindsight, really did need some help, and it wasn't going to happen in that place. I was lucky. I was quite intelligent compared to the others; they had no education and didn't want any. Borstal to them was a badge of honour. They got their mark under their left eye, like a blue stamp — just a dent — but that's how you know where people have been.

Anyway, I digress. Back at school and time to knuckle down to my best subjects. These were spelling, reading, maths, and mental arithmetic. I had a gift for working things out in my head with tremendous ease, thinking ahead. I suppose that's why I was always in trouble first. I could get into trouble at school before I left home. Now that's a gift.

We had a test each week on different subjects, and whoever came out on top became a monitor, a bit like a teacher's pet, for that week. I won it once, and I made sure it would never happen again. It's the worst job in class. You do all the messages for those bone-idle sods and hand the milk out at playtime. Now that's one job you don't want. The bottles are wet, cold, smelly, and the milk sticks to you all day, and when it starts to go off, so do you.

Nearing the end of my primary education, the last year in class was good for me. I had a good teacher. They called him Mr. Pagendam. He took a shine to me (he must have; he only caned me once a week). I think he felt I had been harshly punished, which in my mind, I was, but on reflection, these things even themselves out. I was out of control and needed to be pulled into line, but I did win the schoolboy of the year award for being the best student. Looking back on it, it was a great honour, and I was chuffed with myself.

After school, we always played football before I went home, as there was no one in anyway; everyone was out or working. I remember coming home early one day and the house was full of women, most unusual. When I walked in, everyone went quiet.

"I need you to go to the local shop for some groceries," my mother said. She railed off a list: bread, butter, boiled ham, cigarettes, "and your father's dead."

So I am walking down the road, going through my mind what the powers that be wanted me to get: bread, butter, boiled ham, cigarettes, and my dad is dead. This just stopped me in my tracks. My dad is dead?

I went back home and asked, "My dad is dead?"

"We will talk about it later. Get yourself away to the shops."

I was in shock. Apparently, he jumped off the back of a bus. In those days, the busses were open at the back. Anyway, he jumped off on a bend as the bus slowed to try to catch another bus before it left the station. As he jumped off, a car from behind hit him. Fortunately, it was outside a hospital and as they rushed him down to theatre, the doctors were not that hopeful. My mother decided to make arrangements for the funeral, trying to plan ahead, but thankfully, my dad pulled through and lived for many years after.

It was not long after that, that my dad's father died. My grand-dad was a miserable old bugger, to me anyway. He had an allotment and I was sent every Sunday to help and to bring home the vegetables. He was always at our house, as he hadn't a television and we had. He would come over, sit down, and tell everyone what we were going to watch.

Quite funny, really, was when he was in the hospital with pneumonia, they thought he was on his last leg. My mother had told the insurance man (who fancied my mum) that my granddad had kicked the bucket, and believe it or not, they paid out. Well, about four weeks later, when the insurance man was on his round, he spots my granddad working in his garden. He was so shocked he went up to Granddad, asked if it was him. "Aren't you dead?" said the insurance man.

The old bugger was so confused, believing he had died and been resurrected, that he just walked off and said nothing, so the insurance man approached my mum and told her he had seen him when he was walking down the street digging his garden, to which my mum said, "Well. Who have we buried then?"

He couldn't do anything about it; he would have got the sack. There was no death certificate or nothing. How she got paid, we will never know; we know only that she did get paid.

At school, I was studying for my eleven plus. I needed to pass this exam, as I wanted to go to grammar school, and I am not sure why. Nobody in the family was interested in whether I went or not. In fact, nobody in the family ever qualified or passed their eleven plus exam. It wasn't going to be any great shakes; also it was quite expensive, with the uniforms, etc. But to me, it seemed important. The one thing that did strike me: The girls at grammar school seemed so sophisticated. They had long legs, high heels, no knickers, and no spots. They would smoke fags in cigarette holders, as I thought. I found out later they were Tampax pods.

We were so naïve, we thought if you pull the little string attached, the one hanging out their knickers, that they would inflate and push their tits out. After numerous tries, I found out that was a load of crap. It was about that time I realised I was turning into a junior pervert, as we know it today, but to me, it was just a thirst for knowledge. I read the books, leered at the magazines. I had orgasms coming out of my ears, which worried me. People said they usually come elsewhere. I had seen some ugly boys with some lovely girls. It had to be my turn soon, surely.

My first real love, I suppose, was a girl called Janet Harris. She thought I was wonderful, which, of course, I was. I remember taking her to the cemetery for a grope and anything else I could get. We were both lying on the grass next to a gravestone, and my hand started to wander. I just had this urge to grope her breasts, feel her nipples, the usual for a horny young chap like me. The problem was she didn't have any (breasts, that is), and there's me lying there for three hours waiting for her to breathe out. My mum's ironing board wasn't as flat as she was. She said she had something in her bag for me. I thought, *I bet it's not a pair of tits.* She produced a ring (not what you're thinking — that would have been magnificent!).

She said we were engaged now and asked when I would be giving her a ring. Well, the one thing we didn't have at home was a phone, but somehow I don't think that's what she meant. I thought, *Where on earth am I going to steal one of them from?* This was to be continued.

At last, my luck was about to take a massive turn. My face and name were in the local paper, along with my school, for all the right reasons. I had been asked to attend the county and North of England football trials. This was, as I have already stated, a great honour for me, which extended to the girls, who were now interested in me, a "celebrity." I was an A-lister.

I would get my fair share of girls because I was such a good foot-baller, and local clubs wanted me to sign with them. As I said, it soon got round that there was a future star in their presence, but the girls were way out of my league. I think I became, to them, just a fashion accessory. They were all from well-to-do families, and most of them had their own front-door key. The only thing I had of our front door was the letterbox. My mother used to hang the key to the house behind the letterbox on about two hundred feet of elastic. By the time you managed to pull all the elastic through with this bloody key on the end, you would be halfway down the street and the rest of the family would have arrived home. If the cat felt playful, you could spend all day and never get the bloody thing out at all.

Back to my story and to primary school. This, somehow, I forgot to mention. I had the distinctive honour to be only the second boy — and I believe to this day I am still only the second boy — to have represented the school with honours for football at a local, county level. But the biggest achievement was when I was chosen to trial for the North of England schoolboys. This achievement especially, and the honours I received on behalf of the school, got me out of all sorts of scrapes. Football was and still is my great passion. The trials took place in Bradford, under fifteens, under eighteens, and under twenty-ones. We played in a competition against the Germans, the Scots, and the Irish. It was most unusual for a football trial, and I have had a few. We were given medals and badges. It probably wouldn't mean a lot today, when kids as young as eight are having trials for big clubs. The money in football now is just obscene. It goes only to the big clubs; the lower league clubs get virtually nothing, even though that's where the investment should be, to allow kids to improve and make a name for themselves while helping the smaller clubs in the process. It's a greedy game run by greedy people.

I had a nice time at school. I was voted Most Outstanding Pupil when I left primary school. We had an honours board, and I was the only person — along with a boy ten years earlier, called Alan Cooper — on that board. Now *that* I was proud of, and to this day I still am.

Before starting grammar school, I had the summer holidays to contend with: Six glorious weeks earning pocket money, stealing golf balls and apples, and, the most lucrative, returning pop bottles. This in itself was very lucrative. You used to get three pence on an empty pop bottle. They used to store them in the back of the shops and the off licences. At night, we would relieve them of their bottles, without them knowing, of course, and relay them back round to the front to get our ill-gotten gain.

This money we used for fags, pictures, and the odd bottle of beer, which as youngsters, we were trying for the first time. It's quite strange how something could taste so obnoxious that people would pay money for it.

Talking about paying for things, Saturday evenings and Sundays, I used to do a job for one of the girls on the docks, showing sailors where she lived. They would give me two shillings and sixpence, then would go in a room and she would tell them to wash. As they were in the throes of showering, she would run like hell out the other door, and give me sixpence. I would run one way and she'd go another. It was quite lucrative, but bloody dangerous. As a kid, you don't view danger if you think you're doing nothing wrong and getting paid for it. On reflection, I was bloody lucky I never got caught.

Back to the beer, a liquid that scrambled your brains and took control of your mouth, not to say your stomach's contents and your legs. It was quite funny; you would get up to leave and your legs would say, "Where's he going? I am not ready yet," and just simply refuse. In the end, your body went one way, the rest of you the other. You became a rag doll. They say drugs get you high, but enough alcohol does exactly the same. You feel like Superman, a tough guy; you make rash promises, and in return for this ludicrous behaviour, you end up throwing up somewhere and counting the cost. I had seen all this in my brief youth. I saw my dad tie himself with his trouser belt to a lamppost outside our house to sort his money out at the end of a working week, drunk as a lord: This is what was his and what was my mum's housekeeping. This was the only way he could count his money and stay upright. This way, he didn't fall over. It's strange. It was the same lamppost we used to get our electric from six months of the year, till the bastards moved it.

My dad always professed to be a social drinker. My mother said he couldn't pass a pub without going in and being sociable, as he felt it was an insult to the landlord — even if he didn't know him — and a bigger insult if he came home before closing time, but I loved him.

Our local was called the Brown Cow, an odd name for a pub, but it's where everyone congregated on a Saturday night, playing darts, cards, dominoes. The men had the bar side; the lounge part was where the women were taken to relax so the swearing couldn't be heard. Those women could swear. The lounge, or the posh side, as it was called, usually had a stained carpet, where the bar was plain and simple, with ordinary sawdust on the floor. That was so the blood wouldn't stain the floor. We used to look through the window at the old women. Once they had a drink, they didn't care. Legs akimbo, they wore the strangest underwear: large, small, some not at all. God, they looked ugly. The ones with no knickers on, all you could stare at was hair, and lots of it. No teeth in; it put me off sex for a good five minutes.

To earn extra money, I used to help my brother on his window-cleaning round. He was a grafter; at least, that's what he told me. It must have been tough for him, holding the ladders while I climbed up and cleaned those bloody windows. We got chased a couple of times. Once, when I was up the ladder cleaning the window of one house; it was really a bad one, but by the time I finished, it was sparkling, and all of a sudden, here is this old lady. She must have been at least 117, on this commode; well, she sees me and screams, getting off the commode, not knowing whether to wipe her bum or pull her knickers up. What a size! Pull them up! She could have camped in them, or at least wiped her arse. Her son comes running out. I say running, as fast as you can with a Zimmer frame, calling us Peeping Toms and saying he was going to report us to the local police. Well, we took off, or my brother did; he just left me with the ladder, bucket, chammy leather, and change of address. The village was quite odd, but unique; it was named Port Sunlight. Quite an incredible place.

Our next clash with our customers was when we were cleaning leaded windows. I did a good job, I thought, till one customer chased us down the street, threatening bodily harm. The lead went onto the glass, leaving him to, as he said, live in the blitz — everything was blacked out.

We thought as we were getting such a good name, it would probably be wiser to move territories. We went to Spital; that's were the upmarket people lived. We had this one house, and as it ended up, it was the only one. I was up the ladder about to clean this window, and it had lace curtains, so you had to get up close to make sure you were doing a proper job. Then I saw it; I'd read about it and heard about it, but never believed it. This woman was riding an exercise bike with no saddle and no clothes on, looking in a large mirror. Well, every time she pedalled, something strange was disappearing up her bum. I told my brother to come and have a look. He couldn't get up those ladders quick enough.

Rung by rung, on foot, hand, and shoulder, and when he saw what I had been whispering about, he turned. Then I turned and the ladder turned, and we went arse over tit through this greenhouse. Thank God it wasn't glass, but the noise was just horrendous. We left the ladder, running down the street, laughing or hysterical, and that, folks, was the end of a very unsuccessful business.

I wouldn't mind — the ladders were not ours — but the memory lingers on to this day. If that woman is still alive and this book gets published, she will if she buys it know who she was, and may I say, you made a young man unbelievably happy. Thank you, and … er … you owe us for a set of ladders.

CHAPTER 4
Cherry Popped

I was nothing startling at grammar school. Academically, I wasn't going to set the world alight. I got through it best I could, and when I left, the headmaster gave me a Bible. I didn't know if it was his way of thanking God I was leaving or just praying that was the last he'd see of me.

Teachers are a strange lot. They fill you full of shit when you're at school, and then say you will amount to nothing when you leave. They are suspicious of everything you do and don't do. You surely have to have a split personality to be one of them. I can't complain. I got away with more than I got caught with.

I got away with a lot of things because I was a first-class athlete. It sounds like I am blowing my own trumpet, but I was a first-class athlete. I played for the school rugby, cricket, athletics, and boxing teams, but my forte was I was a very good footballer, with lots of clubs interested in signing me. I eventually went to my local club, Tranmere Rovers, and played for the youth teams, which then were called Prenton Park Rovers. I collected a few honours, played for and captained Cheshire County, but my biggest honour, as I have already mentioned, was North of England against the Scots, Germans, and Irish at a place called Bradford Park Avenue. When you approach the stadium, you look down on it and it's the only bit of green in Bradford.

I asked myself if the adult world was now ready for me. I was not sure. I was still a virgin, but events were about to change my life dramatically. I was about to become a man. I think it was the summer of 1962.

This was the year, the next dramatic time in my life: losing my virginity at fourteen, way under the pier at New Brighton. Believe me, it was not easy.

I was working on the fairground in New Brighton. There was an indoor and outdoor fairground, and both were great fun. On the outdoor, I worked for an Irish family looking after the stalls. On the indoor, it was a London-based company. There, I worked on the rides, and that's where you made the money. The ride called the Waltzer was the best. It used to fly around at breakneck speed. We would bounce the Waltzer up and down, and the money used to drop out of the punters' pockets, down the back of the Waltzer and into a little tray underneath. At the end of the night, we would split the cash. The ride was also perfect for picking up girls. It was brilliant.

Underneath the fairground was an underground bar called the Creep In, and boy, was it creepy. It was like tunnels going everywhere and was dark as hell. I met this lovely girl from Wolverhampton who had taken a shine to me. She thought I was the bees' knees. After spending most of the day with her, that evening, we ended up on the beach under the pier. My heart was racing.

She asked, "What's that noise?"

Well, I just couldn't answer. I just felt, all of a sudden, that the time was right. My problem was, I always thought the time was right and it never was. I decided to surrender my body and give myself to this buxom beauty. Her name escapes me for the moment.

As I remember, there was a lot of her, and being young and desperate, I wanted it all. The last time I'd had so much excitement was on the same beach eight years earlier, when my mother had just knitted me a brand-new pair of woollen trunks. These were both colourful and life threatening, and when you went swimming in them, once wet, it was like wearing lead weights. You got in okay, and they certainly kept you steady — you know, like an anchor. Getting out, that was another story. Here is me, three stone, and the trunks at least three stone when wet. The crotch used to drop to your knees, holding about eight gallons of water. Getting out with them on was like rescuing a sack of coal, and the silly sods thought you looked nice in them. You looked like a refugee. And those sandwiches they used to make, supposedly fresh. … They were always egg and always full of sand, and that was before you got to the beach.

I shouldn't complain really. A good mate of mine, who should remain nameless, his parents used to take him to Southport Beach. That's where the tide used to take a week to come in. They used to say it was the turds holding it back. Like the Mersey, it was the only river where the seagulls wore protective clothing and the rats ran around in Wellington boots and rubber gloves. The only chance you had of getting wet was in the toilets, but once there, his parents must have been the eternal optimists. They used to put his bathing trunks on him and give him a pair of binoculars, not forgetting his egg-and-tomato-sand sandwiches and those fucking deck chairs made in Japan. They were designed to stop you going to the beach. You got a headache trying to erect them, you got a backache sitting in them, and it was a ball-ache trying to get out of them. And then some cheeky bastard charged you for the privilege.

Back to my deflowering. There we are, under the pier. It's getting quite dark and I am getting quite excited. She's lit a fag, all romantic; the stage is set. I thought, *Well, I will start with a bit of French kissing* while at the same time dusting the fag ash off my shoulder. I shuddered to a halt.

I thought, *Shoulder? I am taller than she is. Shit.* I realise I am sinking. The sand is giving way beneath my feet. I am hanging on to her the best I can, sliding past her breasts, bashing my ear against her nipples, tongue slipping down her tummy, with her knickers in my hand, past her belly button, past the bikini line, and then it appears before me … heaven's carpet. It was just hair at first, and there was a lot of it. In fact, at that moment, it could have been another head; its mouth seemed big enough. Then I stopped, thank God, and climbed back up.

She must have thought, *How's he doing all this without a ladder?* Then she said in that romantic voice, "Are you going to be long?"

Well, my scrotum was asking the same question. Anyway, with trembling hands and everything else, I dipped my penis into the wishing well of life. Ahh. My next stutter. I was a stud. I raised myself to my full height eventually, brushed some more ash out of my hair and off my shoulders, and smiled. I felt fantastic.

She said, "Are we ready to start?"

I thought, *Start? What sort of woman are you?* I mean, she still hadn't finished her cigarette. Here I am, standing there, knees soaking wet. I had already finished, had something to eat, and was heading for the bus home. It was going to be another couple of years to my next erotic experience.

She was very experienced, had it all: her own home, large breasts, tattoos, moustache, and one ear. She had about eight kids. You didn't as much penetrate her as you went in first for a look around to see if it was empty. She asked me if I was taking precautions.

Well, after viewing what was on offer, I had no choice. I said, "Yes, don't worry. I have tied my feet to the bottom of the bed."

She said, "Don't be stupid," and enquired if I had any Durex or rubbers.

I didn't have a clue about them — had never seen one, never worn one. I said, "I don't know what you mean."

She said, "You know, French letters."

I thought, *Shit, is she asking for references?*

She appeared to be a friendly girl, or at least the six fathers of her eight children must have thought so. She had a heart of gold and a fanny to match. She had a tattoo on her inner thigh that said, "This way up," with an arrow pointing toward her private parts. I mean, who gets something like that? Maybe it should have read, "Wear your hard hat before entering." This was all new to me and, I have to say, fascinating.

She was my first introduction to oral sex. It's the only time I can honestly say I wish I wore a mask. She made me feel like a shampoo bottle. It wasn't just my tongue she was after; it was my head and shoulders. Every time she breathed in, I felt this strange tug on my ears. I felt a bit like a baby, only I was breech, going in. They have never been the same since — my ears, that is. I can remember asking her if she had climaxed, as my ears were getting wet and it echoed. Can't remember the reply. I was too busy trying to unblock my bubbling ears.

When the kids rushed in the room, and they often did, it was like having an audience. I can remember her saying, "Send what's-his-name for cigarettes."

I thought, *Shit, how many has she got that she can't even remember the poor buggers' names?*

She turned to me and said, "Should we try again?"

Well, I was astonished. I hadn't stopped. I can remember saying to my mate, "I think I lost a shoe up there."

He said, "You should have been here last week. My mate lost a crate of Guinness."

I said, "You know her, then?"

He said, "I must say, I have had my moments."

I thought, *I have never heard it called that before, and I hope she does not expect me to bring alcohol. I was drunk just on the experience.*

She was okay, really. She was a cross between Nicole Kidman and a bus accident. She had Nicole Kidman's mole on her thigh. I remember going there one Wednesday night and she called me upstairs. There she was, lying naked on the bed, and in all fairness, there was a lot of her, and it was a big bed. She had nothing on except this bowler hat covering her fanny.

She said, "Do you know what's under here?"

I thought, *Fuck, somebody's fallen in, committed suicide, maybe.* Then I thought, *No, he's obviously gone in backward or got stuck coming out.* Looking around, I thought, *Hello, he must have kept his shoes on. What a hero.*

To be honest, it looked like she was giving birth to a flour-grader and she was going to use me as a sort of mid-husband. Anyway, we didn't have to rescue anyone. When she took the hat away, I saw she had shaved and shaped her pubic hair into my initials. I ask you my initials? My first thought was blackmail. My second thought was sectioning, and she should have been.

I said, "How did you do that?"

"In the mirror. Why?"

I said, "It's back to front and upside down. It looks like one of those mazes you get lost in, a bit like Hampton Court."

I should have realised when she first took advantage of me that there was something wrong. Listen to this. She said she had twins. One was sixteen, the other eighteen. Bearing in mind you're explaining this to a person with a grammar school education and one not completely stupid. We did study biology in school. To be fair, you could have painted her orange and she still wouldn't look any brighter. It's also a fact that the inside of her fanny was like a builders' yard, but surely a child couldn't get lost in there for two years. Or could it? Fuck knows how old that flour-grader was.

I had come to the conclusion it wasn't so much a fanny as a work of art. It was great for hiding things in, but it didn't provide the confidence a young boy like me needed. The rope burns around my ankles were turning septic. When I went to see the doctor about them, he asked me if I had been tied up or kidnapped. You cannot say, "No, I was having sex and taking precautions," can you? It was either the headboard or invest in a pair of skis.

I had to end this relationship. I couldn't be associated with her any longer. Her demands sexually were making me paranoid. My body didn't need to be more flexible or broken in about fourteen places. She wanted three in a bed, every man's dream, but there was just no way I could get that fucking donkey up them stairs. Oh, yes. I didn't realise she was an animal lover. She told me once that if I'd tie a brick on the end of my cock, it would make it bigger (that fills you with confidence). I thought, *Brilliant* (Who needs a grammar school education? What a waste!), *maybe I can get one from her builders' yard.* I can just see me walking round all day with this house brick hanging from my old man, crotch down to my knees, bashing it against dustbins, ringing bells.

And this woman was bringing innocents into the world. Their education would surely be a sight to behold. I am not sure she gave birth. I think they just sent in search teams every nine months.

As I say, I had to end this friendship or my street credibility would have gone right down the pan. At least I learned from our brief experience and realised that not all lunatics are locked up. But as an up-and-coming gigolo, you need these older, experienced woman to show you the ropes, and she did — and the knots to go with them. I remember her once tying me to the bed and asking me what I would like her to do next. All I could think of was, *Call a taxi.*

The best part of growing up sexually is what you teach yourself, hand jobs, and the best of all, your imagination. When God made us, He surely gave us this wonderful gift of imagination. It makes men invincible and women phenomenal.

CHAPTER 5

My First Holiday

My first flight, I was fifteen and flew out of Liverpool to Jersey. It was a holiday to see my brother, who lived and worked there — a beautiful place — but the plane they put us on was, to say the least, limited. Dan Dare Airways — and I thought that was a cartoon. I never in my wildest dreams imagined I would be appearing in one. The wings flapped and, shit, they did. It was a race to see who was up a height first, the aircraft or us.

In those days, the safety talk was quite brief. It went like this: "In the event of us crashing into the sea, undo your seat belt, lean forward, place your head between your legs, and kiss your arse goodbye." This was followed by: "Today's food will be served if we have time. Anyone ordering wine, please ensure you have a bottle opener with you, and get into the holiday spirit and pass it around (the bottle opener). Please, when using the toilets, sit; do not stand, as the urine trickles onto the flight deck, and this really pisses the captain off. If we are running late, we will tell you upon arrival."

Now that, in general, was it. You would have gotten better service from the Luftwaffe.

I had a real nice holiday in Jersey, and in later years spent some summers there, working and lazing about; beachcombing; checking the beach for valuables when the holiday-makers had left; finding goodies, money, jewellery, used condoms, egg sandwiches (which rings a bell). One thing about Jersey, the women were wonderful. They outnumbered the men by about three to one. I was quite lucky in that department. I had quite a few girlfriends, but sexually, I was still missing out.

I picked up this beautiful girl called Jenny, who had a sister called Penny (no, it's not a rhyme). I was back at the guest house where they were staying with their parents, and Jenny and I were on the bed. I was just about to pounce when we heard Penny coming through the door and up the stairs. This was a family room, and I didn't know it at the time, but we had been on top of their parents' bed.

Now I am under it, Penny is stripping, and I can see these long legs, but I cannot see enough. I can hear her talking, bra hitting the floor, then knickers hitting the floor. By this time, I am so excited I have this urge to look. Just as I was about to peek, in walk Mum and Dad.

Now, you have to understand. This bed is quite close to the floor, with only enough room for me and a couple of suitcases. It has a mattress and a spring, so when the mother, being quite large, sits on the bed, I am face-to-face with the bedsprings. Then the father joins her and I go from being half a metre wide to a metre wide and breathless. I have to lie there very still, motionless, till everyone has gone to sleep, and figure a way out of this difficult situation without waking anyone up.

I eventually slide out from under the bed as her father goes for a pee in the middle of the night; I'm out the door, down the stairs, into the street. I fill my lungs full of fresh air, not feeling too good. I had difficulty breathing, so on the way home, I went to the hospital, and the nurse said, "What happened to you?" I was struggling to respond, so she sent for the doctor, and I heard him say, "Which one is it," referring to me.

She said, and this came as a shock, "The one in the end cubicle who looks like he's been hit with a chip basket."

Well, if you could see my face! It looked like someone had prepared me for orienteering, my face being the map. It had so many crosses on it that it looked like something out of "spot the ball." I now know how Humpty Dumpty felt. It must have taken the blood two days to get me back together. Another lesson learned. I never got caught like that again. If they wanted sex, it was on my terms or they didn't get it. Consequently, I didn't have a lot of sex.

Now, reading this, you might think this is only about sex and a young lad trying to make his way in life. You would, of course, be right. When you're a young lad, there really is nothing else.

I spent a few years in Jersey, seven in total, I think. My next exciting job, believe it or not, was in a bar, in a place called La Corbier. There, I was to meet a woman who was, by today's standards, extremely wealthy. She used to drink pink gin and get pissed quite easily, and she loved young boys. I was told about her, as I was the new boy on the block, and that if she liked me, she would wink at me after she ordered her drink.

Well, one pink gin coming up, madam. There it was, this famous wink, so I told everyone. They said, "If you play your cards right, you may never have to work again."

Anyway, she took a shine to me, got me pissed one night on red wine, and took me home. I don't really know if anything happened, and that's the truth. I just cannot remember. I do remember waking up in the morning covered in makeup and false eyelashes (well, I knew they were not mine), and smelling of fish and chips. With one eye open, to make sure I had no hangover, I noticed, of all things, to my surprise, chip papers on the bed and a wooden leg in the corner, standing up on its own. I kid you not. I thought, *Fucking hell! Where on earth have I landed?*

I laid back and thought about it for a minute, had another peek, and sure enough it was definitely a wooden leg. Without glancing at my bed partner, I slipped my hand under the bedsheet, and I started a count: one, two (they were mine, I hoped), three. I could only feel three legs. Now, I wasn't in the best state of mind, but I am fucking sure I came to bed with at least two of them. Now, maths being my best subject at school, it didn't take me long to figure out that I wasn't sleeping with the sister of Long John Silver. This was no pirate; this was not a woman with one hairy leg and one clean-shaven leg. This was an "I can never show my face in Corbier again" leg.

It was quite a fun pub, really. The staff were great, took the piss out of the customers like you wouldn't believe. We had one guy who was a regular called François. We were given instructions never to give him alcohol. Fancy telling a young, idiotic crew like we were not to give someone alcohol without telling us why. To us, it was an experiment, and we had to find out.

One weekend when the owners were away, in walks François, in his French beret and wide-awake trousers. It's his lucky night. He can have what he wants, free of charge. After a few wines — music playing, the bar quite busy — François decides he would like to dance and asks this woman of about sixty to dance with him, and she obliges. François starts to get all excited and strip. We panic. We cannot stop him. A lot of the locals are giving him all the encouragement he needs.

Cut to the chase, he's down to his underpants. What wasn't growing out of these was nobody's business. In fact, it was like a mini allotment; even the colour was strange. I cannot honestly say I never recognised what colour they were; they were a sack colour and full as well. I do know that when he took them off and threw them in the corner, they cracked, and there, hanging between his legs, was his masterpiece. And fuck was it! There it was, the biggest cock on the planet, a monster. I have never seen anything so deformed or so big, and that was just François. He wasn't born with this. He must have given birth to it. It wasn't a penis; it was an offensive weapon. All it needed was sights on the end. It was like a baby's arm holding a Jaffa orange. There was a rumour going round that every time he had an erection, he fainted; apparently, there just wasn't enough blood for the both of them.

The owner found out and we were all given notice, which didn't really surprise us, as the owner was from Southampton and a former football referee. We're talking here of sense of humour bypass. I only ever saw him smile once, but my mate said he didn't — it was wind. His wife was quite nice. She liked to give all the boys a full medical every Monday morning when he was at the cash-and-carry.

She was one for really strange sexual habits. She used to get you in bed, get you all excited, then just when you were about to blow everything clean, she would stop, produce this gadget shaped like a pig's tail, and ask you to wear it. Not on your head, as such — on your cock. When you asked the stupidest of questions ("Why?"), she said she had an itch that really needed scratching. Well, if you had seen the size of this thing on the end of your cock, the itch must have been just behind her tonsils. It used to leave awful ring marks on your bell end, and deep, and these ring marks didn't go so quick.

One cheeky woman who saw them said to me, "Do you wrap a piece of string on that to get it started? You know, like an outboard motor, or do those rings tell your age?"

I thought, *That's all I need, a fucking female comedienne,* so I thought no more medicals; stuff the job.

My next job in Jersey was in an animal feed factory. It had every lunatic known to man working in there. I will explain. When God in His wisdom created the earth and then created the countryside, then decided He needed to put something on Earth, He thought of man, and what a brilliant idea. Obviously, every now and then, the odd mistake would come along — you know, women. God called these odd mistakes "walk-offs." Well, while He was putting man and woman together — legs, body, arms, heart, head — just as He was about to put the brains in, a disaster occurred on Earth.

So, He went down to sort it out; once He was away, these human experiments waiting for their brains walked off. Hence, their name, "walk-offs," and the fuckers ended up in this animal feed plant working with me.

These buggers had to lump fifty-kilo sacks of wheat, maize, milo, all sorts of products. They were big and hairy-arsed, with muscles in their spit, and would go for a week unshaven, and the fellas were the same.

The place was full of mice and rats, and the rats were huge. Even the cats were frightened of them. They would stroll round the place in bovver boots without a care in the world. That's the rats. The cats would just hide. They would never attack you. They had too much to eat, and it was quite strange. Where there were rats, there were no mice, and vice versa.

We worked there four days a week, and on a Friday, we used to go up to the farm at a place called Le Galle. The company had battery hens. For the less intelligent reading this book, they were real. There were no switches to them. Now, these poor buggers were kept in the dark (a bit like us, really), in cages twenty-four hours a day, and they would constantly lay eggs. They must have had an arse like a bowling lane.

Friday, we would collect as much guano as possible (to the less initiated, this was hen shit), get the eggs from the battery hens, roll them in hen shit, and box them up so the company could sell them as free-range eggs. You see, free range were far more expensive than battery eggs. It was quite funny. I worked with an Irish guy called Calum. He used to stamp the eggs with the words "free range" before they went into the boxes. One day, the boss gave him a week's notice for constant lateness, so Calum, pissed off, decided to get his own back. He made a stamp that said "yolk-free and overpriced" and stamped about one thousand eggs.

Talk about a steward's inquiry! Everybody was a potential perpetrator, according to the bosses. Even the bloody hens were lined up and questioned and put in what they thought was an identity parade or an escape committee. It was so funny; you just had to be there. The only ones that looked guilty were those bloody chickens, and they were looking at each other as if to say, "It wasn't me. I was playing golf."

We spent the whole of Saturday night in one of the most prestigious stores in Jersey trying to track down over one thousand eggs, and a Saturday night in Jersey was a fun night, so we all ended up being pissed off by Calum and getting pissed in this superstore. This superstore was one of those that sold almost everything, and I found a bottle of Japanese rice wine, or sake, as it's known.

I just had to try it, and I must admit, it certainly helped with my education. I now know why those buggers are miserable little bastards. Who ever dreamed that concoction up? It should have had a skull and crossbones on the bottle. It's got to be the worst drink on God's Earth. I understand now why sumo wrestlers don't drink. It's obviously easier to become thirty stone, wear a nappy, throw salt over your shoulder, and be a sex symbol to a buffalo. It's like sheep's breath; it's served in small cups because they know no one in their right mind would drink it out of anything bigger. Give me the raw fish any day.

One of the strangest experiences I had whilst in Jersey was when a friend of mine (we will call him Jimmy), who I worked with in the animal feed factory, He was a giant ideal if you needed any artexing he was that tall, If he fell over he would have been halfway home, Jimmy wanted to venture out on his own and try his hand at smallholding. His uncle rented him a piece of land and Jimmy decided he was going to be the next pig-farming baron. The only problem was, he had no pigs. In Jersey, there is no such thing as stealing; the phrase used is "borrowing without the owner's consent," so we borrowed this pig, stuck it in a wheelbarrow in the dead of night, and ran like the clappers to Jimmy's smallholding. Christ, are those things noisy when they are woken up! Not to say miserable. There wasn't one sound this bugger didn't make. Anyway, it was a successful pig-napping.

The next thing we needed to borrow was a boar so we could mate Miss Piggy and create more Miss Piggies. This wasn't going to be easy. Those boars never slept. The one we tried to borrow without the owner's permission was a nightmare; it shouted and screamed and squealed so that we coerced it with food. Now, the sow we had was no beauty, but in the pig world may have been Miss Jersey, so as I say, we coerced them into eating the goodies we had brought. Jimmy says, "You get hold of it and I will put a bag over its head."

I thought, *A bag over its head? It hasn't seen the sow yet. It may be easier to get it there and put the bag over the sow's head.*

This was going to be a nonstarter. We were going to have to hire one of these, which meant spending money, something Jimmy's religion was against, a bit like Jehovah's Witnesses only tighter. Jimmy was so tight you could hear his shoes squeak when he walked. Anyway, he went into debt (he sold something he had borrowed earlier).

For this boar to have its leg over was going to cost five pounds, but it was guaranteed it would do the business. Now, the thing about a pig is, when the act has been committed and the sperm accepted, the following day, the pig lies on its side. If it's not on its side, it means it hasn't taken, so you have to try again. Well, the boar does, at — thank God — no extra cost.

This is where the story becomes quite farcical. We go to the farm, the pig's running round. We phone the owner of the boar to tell him the pig is not lying on its side. Shergar (that's the name of his boar) had failed to impress Miss Piggy. He told us to put the pig in the wheelbarrow and wheel her down, and we would try again. This we did.

The next day, the same. Jimmy phones the farmer, puts the pig in the wheelbarrow, takes her to the farm, leaves it for an hour. The boar has a good shag. We take the pig back home and wait. This bloody thing has now had three good shags. We are totally fucking taking, or should I say chauffeuring, this pig back and forward like a pimp.

Next day, I phoned Jimmy and said, "Guess what."

He said, "The pig's lying on its side?"

I said, killing myself laughing, "No, she is not on her side."

"What then?" came the reply.

I said, "She's sitting in the wheelbarrow."

No, that's a joke. The pig is going crazy, running at the wall at full pelt and crashing her head into this concrete pillar, so we get Shergar's owner to come and see what's going on. He brings the boar to the smallholding, thinking it may work better in the pig's own environment. We try to calm the pig down, which we do, then we let the boar in. While we're all watching these two making up, as the boar mounts the pig, the farmer notices the boar is about an inch and a half short of getting it in. He said, "Short back."

We said, "What?"

He said, "Short back. That was the problem."

The boar needed help. Imagine being wound up by your favourite beau, horny as hell, and he cannot do the business. You would be looking for a divorce. We had to build a ramp for the boar, and if you could have seen the expression on that boar's face when he finally got where he was going! It was pure ecstasy. We all breathed a sigh of relief, except Jimmy. I think he came in his pants. We decided to celebrate with a beer, a couple of beers to exact, and go down to the beach for a BBQ and to people-watch.

It's funny watching the locals in the harbour with their rods in hand. I mean, give a man a fish and he will eat for a day, teach a man to fish and he will sit in a boat all day drinking beer. We can be strange creatures. It's said if you line up all the cars in the world end to end, some idiot would be stupid enough to try and overtake.

The sow that Jimmy had was about to give birth, and we were there all night. Well, they started popping out one after another.

After about twelve, they were still coming. If I didn't know better, I would have said he had been shopping for them. There were a total of seventeen, amazing. About five were no good; they were called runts. They either had no legs or two heads. I will say this for the sow: for such a big animal in such a small, confined space, she never stood on any of them. Quite incredible.

I was getting a bit bored with the job and decided I wanted to leave. I mentioned it to the boss, so he got me out driving, making deliveries to the farms with the Jersey drivers, humping fifty-kilo sacks of animal feed to the farms, being chased by bulls, geese, rabid dogs. But they always gave you something, the farmers. Food or eggs, their wives' cups of coffee or brandy, the daughters. Usually a dose of something, and not medicine, I can assure you.

In general, I was quite liked. I got on well at work, represented the company in local football matches, always turned up and worked till we finished. Typical of cargo day, we usually had three hundred tons of maize or milo or wheat to tip by hand. The company fed you and gave you a crate of beer to keep the dust down, but real hard graft. I really did need a change.

It was time to go home. I needed a break from Jersey and pig-wifery, and Jersey needed a break from me. I had reached eighteen, old enough to go in pubs, though I had been doing that since I was fourteen. It's quite strange when you reach eighteen years old. As a tradition, your parents give you the key to the door, and I received mine along with a board increase and about two hundred feet of elastic still attached to the letterbox in which the key was kept.

I had a job at a car factory not far from where we lived. This lasted about a year (before I went back to Jersey); I made cars on the assembly line, but I just couldn't hack it. I played football for them for a while, hoping that would give me some freedom, but that wasn't the case. I remember getting my brother a job there, but he had his own agenda. From the amount of gear he borrowed, he must have had his own shop. I used to pick him up after his shift was finished and he would walk out like a robot, rigid from the amount of stuff hidden under his jacket and down his trousers. It was amazing. He couldn't sit down in the car. I used to stand him up, push him over, slide him in the back seat, and try to shut the door. He was like a human magpie, nicking all these car parts from the factory. I wouldn't have minded, but he didn't even have a vehicle.

A year had gone by and I just couldn't settle, so I returned to Jersey and my old job with the animal feed manufacturer. The staff hadn't changed; the walk-offs didn't get any brighter, except one called Strange Brian. They called him that because he was. He had the strangest way about him. He had one big eye and one little eye, and when he answered a question or laughed, they looked at each other. He was no designer baby, that's for sure, but you could talk to him. He wouldn't fucking listen or answer, but you could talk to him. The nearest thing to sanity was a lad called Neville. He was a typical Jersey boy: never blew his nose. There were always these candlesticks hanging; you could abseil down them. If you tried to have a conversation with him, you had to wear a burkha or you could come away covered in all sorts of bits and pieces, including a bucketload of snot, and you invariably did. He was as strong as an ox, muscles in his spit; slept with his sister till she got pregnant, and Neville's sister was no beauty. The only way you would get me to sleep with her would be in a coma and wearing that burkha.

We came to the conclusion that the baby couldn't have been Neville's. If it was, she must have helped herself during the night. He thought it was for pissing through and digging up clams, which will give you an idea of its shape and size. He had two teeth that were his own, and quite a funny-shaped head. It's something I didn't really notice that much till his dad came to work one day and asked, "Is Peanut about?"

I thought, *Peanut?* I had never heard anyone called that.

He said, "Neville. I am Neville's father."

Then it struck me. I thought, *Fucking hell! What a shame. His head could have been built by headcase homes because they can't get anything right either.* He was so embarrassed I thought, *I won't tell anyone,* then I thought I might, then I thought, *Fuck it. I will.*

Meantime, Calum was back on the scene. Not exactly back, but in Newgate Street Prison. To this day, I don't know what he did, but he was a bit of a wise guy, so it could have been anything, and it wasn't too long before I joined him there. I had this lovely young girl out one night, and we were having a drink in the Goblet Bar. This was just a long, straight bar: one way in and one way out. I am telling her how wonderful I am and how lucky she may be to have me later on. Then a fight breaks out, and as the fighters were making their way along the bar, I was trying to push her over the bar out of the way. The barman was having none of this and was pushing her back. Next thing, I am hit with a chair.

There I am, flat on my arse, trying to get up and get some protection for us both out of this melee, when I had this searing pain in my backside. It was my steel comb. As I was trying to get it out, someone shouted, "He has got a knife." Next thing I knew, I was on the floor in the back of a Jersey police wagon. To cut a long story short, there was court the next morning, I wasn't allowed to speak, and the judge said three months, take him down. Now, they had put two stitches in my arse, and they knew I was an innocent bystander. Well, as innocent as I could look.

We arrived straight into administration, and I showered, dressed, got a haircut and fatigues, then moved into my new hotel room in B block, cell 8. The next day, the work detail was chopping wood. I was introduced to the guard, who told me I would be working or assisting a Jock (that is a Scotsman). He said, "Be careful what you say. He is a bit of a lunatic. Shouldn't be in here, really, should be in a psycho ward, but the only mental hospital we have here is short of space."

I thought, *Wonderful.*

What do they do? They give him an axe. I thought, *Shit.* I didn't only think it, I could smell it, and it was definitely mine, as were the tears rolling down my leg. Well, when it comes to health and safety, that just didn't exist. It was: "Hold this log in place while the mad axman tries to hit the log and avoid the digits attached to my hand or shortening my right arm," so speed was of the essence. I worked with him for a week and he went a bit loopy — not, may I add, because he was working with me. He just lost it, ran up to the Wailing Wall, and started shouting expletives as only a Scotsman can when he is sober. He never spoke to me, just burped and grunted. He would have probably been much better off on Jimmy's pig farm.

Breakfast time was a bit strange. The first thing you did was spit on your bread so no one else would eat it. You were not so much on a diet as starved, and you were hungry all day. As far as the food, you had two choices: take it or leave it.

We prepared the wood, and there was lorry loads of the stuff (you would have thought we were building the bridge on the River Kwai). That five weeks I was on the woodpile, I felt like Pinocchio. They thought I was trustworthy and didn't cause any problems, so my new job was as a van assistant, going out with the warders, humping things that those lazy buggers wouldn't hump, like bags of flour or manure for the gardens.

The town hall used to give us jobs to do, like check when the sewers were blocked and pick up rubbish. Down to St. Brelades one day, the local builders were rebuilding a wall that had collapsed onto the beach. They needed a trench dug, so four of us were nominated. We were in this ditch, working hard, doing a bit of sunbathing, and having a smoke when this idiot on a bicycle came tumbling in. Well, by the time the lads had checked his pockets and borrowed his watch, we thought maybe we should call for help. The warders, bless them, were sweating away on the beach, scraping the rust off their handcuffs and making sure the holes in their pockets hadn't been stitched up.

Back to the cyclist. We all lay down, injured and covered in blood (it was his, actually), thinking that's us for a week or two in the hospital infirmary. No such luck. We were back there the next day, up to our plimsolls in mud and bike parts.

The cell was quite comfortable: metal bunk beds, thin mattresses, and even thinner blankets. I was on my own, but lonely. You were lonely, even more so when the cell door locked and the lights went out and it was cold. The only atmosphere was your hot breath into the cold night air. We had a pool table of sorts. It was a Russian billiard table with three wooden men on it, surrounded by holes. We had table tennis with soft bats and table-tennis balls with holes in them. It was like batting with a paper bag. There was visiting once a month, in a room with a huge wooden table so people could pass contraband — cigarettes and food — under it, out of sight of the guards. The guards themselves were friendly enough. It wasn't by all accounts a tough prison; people in there had not really committed serious crimes. It was all petty stuff or fighting, though there was a guy who murdered his sister — buried her alive. But he was segregated. I never saw him, but he was at Coca-Cola when I worked there in the valley. He didn't seem the sort, but there is nothing stranger than folk.

I did ten weeks and was released. I had some time with Calum. I still don't know what he did, but when I left, he was still there. My old boss took me back, but I really needed a break, so I went back to England.

It was 1966, and England was hosting and winning the World Cup. Some thought they recognised me as one of the Mexican World Cup squad. I was seen leaving Goodison Park with my cousin, who was a linguist for the now-named FIFA. He could speak about twenty-five languages. I wasn't going to miss the chance of a free party. They thought I was with the team, and who was I to disappoint anyone? I said I was. Bear in mind that I had to see this through; I needed help and protection. I phoned a few people I could trust and let them know what was happening, and we went partying.

You just would not believe the women that tried to get their hands into my pants. Being a visitor to your country and a slapper, I let them. Unbelievable; my trousers were up and down like a yo-yo. My scrotum thought it had died and gone to Heaven, and in all honesty, if anyone had found out, I would have joined it. The only thing I should have done was charge, but I didn't have it in me.

This wonderful party introduced me to this part-time model called Clair. I found out later it was doorstops she was modelling. She was beautiful, quite a large girl but lovely looking, with a great sense of humour and huge breasts. If you managed to get one in your mouth, you would have to put the other one in a bucket. But trying to get my hands in her knickers was another story. Shit, she must have put them on with a shoehorn. I am not joking.

She said in that sweet, scouse, romantic voice, "Are you going to be long?"

I thought, in all honesty, *I cannot put a time on this. Fucking hell, I need a blowlamp.* I sweated so much trying to get them off, you could have made a pan of chips. It's the only time I have ever given up on a potential screw.

She could see how wound up I was and took pity on me. She said, "I suppose you would like a handjob now, would you?"

I said, "I wouldn't fuckin' mind."

She said, "Carry on. I will be in the bar when you've finished," which just about sums my sex life up.

Back to the story. Having this wonderful erection all evening with all these lovely women around was marvellous. The problem was, I couldn't get it down. Now, you studs out there must be thinking "lucky bastard," but no, I had to go to Clatterbridge Hospital. A muscle had stuck and the blood flowed consequently. It stayed erect; it went black, blue, then purple. At one stage, probably green. I could hardly walk, and pissing was an art. It just wouldn't bend. Having a crap was like being perched on one of these hot geysers; one minute everything was being drawn out of you, and the next, you were ready to blow. I had to stuff my penis in, of all things, a type of petrol can and cling-film it.

I am quite sure that if I could have done handstands, I could have had a decent piss. The nurses thought it was hilarious, me lying there with everything stuck in the air, and they just left me to it. One said, eating a donut, "Would you like me to throw anything over it?"

I thought, *Well, a blanket would help.*

They thought I should be cleaned out, so they introduced me to an enema, something I had never seen or even heard about before, and something I never want again. She came in with this bucket of soapy water and a long lance, Vaseline, and a sickly grin. This nurse was the right one to do it. The look on her face … she could frighten a ghost. My first thought was, *One of us should be wearing armour.* My second thought was, *She might be.*

She said to me in a sickly droll way, "You know where this is going, don't you?"

I thought, *Down the fucking grid, I hope.* I tried in vain to explain to her I was a virgin and it was against my religion to have anything inserted into me without prior notice and an awful lot of money; then a voice from behind said, "Settle down, now. Let's have no tantrums."

Well, if you could have seen the size of him; they must have found him on Halloween or holding up London Bridge. What a monster! He had a huge belly, looked like he had been inserted with a foot pump or maybe was carrying somebody's love child. What a size! It took my mind off the enema — for a couple of seconds, anyway.

Give those nurses their due. If they're having a bad day, they don't muck about. The more pain they can inflict on you, the better.

"Lie on your left side," was the next instruction, then they come at you like a bat out of hell. Shit! That's the only word going through your mind, and the cheeks of your arse are knocking together like they're in a band, a form of clapping or taking deep breaths. They then give you the equivalent of a corned beef tin to sit on till everything you've got has left your body. This, of course, also includes your heart and soul. Your arse feels like somebody's rubbed it with wire wool or sandpaper, then set it alight. This much I can tell you: The only thing to come out of my arse in the days following was a white flag.

My pride and joy was out of action for a month, and so was I. It was an experience I would not want to wish on anyone, but that bastard with the wooden leg comes pretty close.

The next couple of years were a bit mundane, but I was coming up to my 21st birthday. My mum and dad bought me a radiogram. Now, for those times, that was pretty upmarket, and for anybody reading this over the age of 106, you will know what it is: a posh record player with a wireless attached. I was hoping for something smaller, to be honest, but their logic was, the bigger it is … and it was big. I couldn't take it out of the house.

Back to the birthday. I decided to throw a surprise birthday party for me and four mates, which lasted approximately forty minutes, till we ran out of booze. No booze left, we slinked off to some nightclub in Liverpool, the Cavern Club. It was dingy, a bit like an underground railway station, only smaller and not so smelly, but the music was always good and loud. The Cavern, due to the success of the Beatles, became world famous. In all honesty, there were far better groups than the Beatles at that time, but as luck would have it, they became famous, as did the club.

Liverpool, for a capital city (of the north, that is), did not have a lot of nightlife, but the girls, or Judys as they were called, were plentiful. A hell of a lot more than across the water where I had lived. The nearest you ever came to sexual energy was watching two dogs having it off with each other, then going home and throwing it over your thumb, thinking that some girl has just missed out on a magical exhibition — but not about the two dogs, of course.

In those days, we had so much pent-up sexual energy you only had to sneeze to get an erection, so pepper was always kept handy. The girls where I lived were always saving it up for somebody, but never me.

I remember the vicar catching me in one of the pews. (Do these buggers not walk around properly? They just appear out of thin air with their Bible and carpet slippers.) Anyway, there I was, attacking myself with a five-fingered widow. His voice boomed, "What's going on?"

I said, "I'm caught in my zip."

"Oh, yes? What was it doing out in the first place? Were you thinking of taking it for a walk? You must save it up till you meet the right girl."

I didn't have the heart to tell him I had — saved it up, that is — and there were about forty jars of the stuff at home. Shame on me.

It was about this time I got into a loving relationship with a beautiful student nurse called Jacqui at Clatterbridge Hospital. We were really into each other, and the sex was great but long overdue. We practised a lot, did all the experiments that you do, and it was a good learning experiment for both of us. There were no boundaries; anywhere and everywhere. The hospital was where, for the first time, I had sex with a coloured girl, called Dinah. She was gorgeous, covered in freckles, and her tongue was like a cat's tongue, very much like sandpaper. When you finished kissing her, you went home all smooth.

Jacqui was really special. The first time I fell in love, I believe, and we ended up getting engaged. The first time we had sex was at her house, and she was a virgin. All this took place on New Year's Eve; what a way to bring in the New Year.

Her parents were out for the evening, and when they came back, her father said to me, "I hope your intentions toward my daughter are honourable." I thought how strange it was that I had just popped her cherry and he comes out with that.

That evening while we were trying to wear the carpet out, the floor must have been shaking like hell. The prized budgie fell off its perch and lay at the bottom of the cage, dead-o, legs upturned, facing the ceiling. We spent the next half hour gluing the bugger back on its perch. You know, four days went by before they realized it was not of this world anymore. It was stuck on this perch looking like a used Durex with feathers. How could anyone not see it was either dead or depressed?

There was a brief inquiry as to how Joey, that was its name, passed on. When the burial day came (same day; it was a Jewish bird), they couldn't get the little sod off the perch. They were saying, "It doesn't want to leave." To this day, they still don't know why it was stuck. They buried it sideways, still on the perch. Jacqui wrapped it up like it was embalmed.

We celebrated the bird's death. The great thing about nurses, apart from the uniform, is that they know how to party. In a way, we celebrated twice: with her virginity and the bird's death.

Boarding at the hospital was like an army camp. They couldn't get out, so a lot of planning used to take place to get them out. Once out, they could drink, dance, and play — all good teenage fun.

She was ready for a change, so we decided to move to Jersey. We both had good jobs to go to, and we worked hard. We got ourselves a nice place to live, but she got homesick, missed her family and old friends. I loved it, though, so there ended a beautiful friendship.

It was Battle of Flowers time, Jersey's carnival weekend. People came from all over the world to view the floats, which were so inventive. There was lots of sunshine, music, and girls. The beaches were packed. The hotels were full of older woman there without their husbands, just looking for a good time, and girls on their stag nights looking for one more fling. The older women were the best; they knew what they wanted and where they wanted it and how they wanted it. All good fun; no stories to tell. There is something about a married woman's body: the smell, the taste, the warmth, and most of all, the experience. They taught you so much. They wanted to do things with you that they never would with their husbands, and that's sad.

CHAPTER 6

Life in North East

Before I left Jersey, I met a nice girl called Sandra, a Geordie from the wonderful North East of England. She was on holiday with her friend, and I was seriously attracted to her. There is something about the Geordies; they are a nation on their own, hard working, honest, with a great sense of humour. They tell it as it is. Fabulous people. Next to scouses, they are the salt of the earth. Anyway, I met this girl in Jersey who invited me home for the Easter weekend in Newcastle. It was a cold place. It was nearly summer, but in the North East, cold was always expected: winter, spring, autumn, or summer.

That weekend, I met her parents. Her mum was nice and friendly, her father a control freak and a bully. His favourite saying was, "Do as I say, not as I do." I think we both knew from day one we were not going to like each other. He was very strict. It was the Easter weekend, and after meeting her parents, sex was definitely out of the question. Nothing was going to rise in her house. I would have been better in Jerusalem for the Second Coming. Here there wasn't even going to be a first, never mind a second. They were quite religious. Her father used to use the Lord's name a lot, normally after he just fell down for the umpteenth time, pissed. He could drink, and I mean drink anything, from a pint of bitter to a bottle of Old Spice. The Old Spice used to make him throw up a lot, but it smelt nice. She was twenty-eight years old and he ruled with a rod of iron. I think, in general, he just hated his kids, which isn't surprising, as he wasn't too keen on himself, either. He must have got up in the morning, looked in the mirror, and thought, *Shit.*

His wife was lovely. She was just like the woman out of the Alf Garnet TV series, "Till Death Do Us Part." She totally ignored him.

When pissed, his habits were disgusting. He once was so drunk he came downstairs into the kitchen and had a shit in the oven. When we got up the next morning, the place stunk and, of course, no one could figure out where the smell was coming from till lunchtime, and there it was, this strange-looking turd curled up on a tray in the oven, pretending to be a Yorkshire pudding. Horrible, just like him.

His wife was mortified, as were his daughters. For me, as a guest in his house, I thought I had met a genuine lunatic. He should have been sectioned, if you think about it. He had to come downstairs, open the oven door, pull the oven tray out, have a shit, push the tray back, close the oven door, and go back to bed. Amazing — and nothing registered.

The only thing nice about Stan (that was his name) was that when he was asleep, he was about six feet two inches tall, and every inch was horrible: white hair, false teeth, moustache, and boy! As I have already said, could he drink! And I mean anything.

To go a bit further, I really took a shine to Sandra. She was just simply lovely. So I decided to stay in the North East. I found a flat on the coast in Whitley Bay, a lovely place but typical of most affordable resorts: beach, fairground, cheap hotels (unless they thought you had a few bob, then they would put the price up), loads of loud music, and a northeastern wind that could turn you to stone. What used to amaze me was that cold North Sea and how it attracted people to swim in it, mainly children and old people who thought they were lost. It would take them an hour to get in and about two minutes to get out, telling everyone how lovely and refreshing it was. If they could have seen themselves — they came out looking like an oil slick with the flu.

The nearest hotel was the Queens at the bottom of the road. A man called Jinksy ran it: nice guy, ex-RAF, and … guess what … he had a wooden leg. The hotel had a strange clientele. I was in there one Friday afternoon and there was a wake going on. The coffin was open and the guests were very complimentary to the old lady lying there. As the drink began to flow and people were looking the worse for wear, the coffin kept getting moved from one end of the bar to the other. Then the music started to play, and the coffin ended up in the gents' toilet.

People were getting excited with all the drink that was consumed, so up till then, it was good — nice buffet. Nice people, really. Then, suddenly, it just erupted. The man closest to the bar enjoying the food all of a sudden was seen flying through the air, still attached to his chair, with a vol-au-vent in one hand and half a pork pie in the other. He went flying through the window, got up, and walked back into the hotel. After ten minutes, they all kissed and made up and just carried on dancing.

Then there was grab-a-granny night at the Rex Hotel, and *grannies* was right. You could spend half the night looking for one with her own teeth. Those old dears had no shame, but they could show you a good time. They were great fun. Some were known to take their hairnets off if they fancied you.

The relationship was going great with Sandra, and I plucked up the courage to ask her to move in with me. She agreed. Living with her parents, her life was passing her by. In fact, she had no life at all, really, just work and home. So we made plans like two kids. It was exciting and it was good fun.

Being recently divorced and having a real bad time with that coward of an ex-husband, she needed to recharge her batteries, let her hair down, and have some fun — enjoy herself. She told me the day they were agreeing to the divorce that they had two dogs, wire-haired terriers, called Danny and Dusty, and she assumed the dogs would go with her. But, being the arsehole he was, he was arguing they should have one each, even though he couldn't care less. She refused, so as a parting shot, he threw one of the dogs on the fire. That's the sort of bloke he was, an absolute moron, a bully. He'd fight anything that couldn't fight back, like most bullies, really. Anyway, she saved the dog, but what a terrifying and traumatic experience, and not just for those dogs.

Funny, really. I'll tell you what kind of coward he was. When she moved in with me, he was watching her (bear in mind they were divorced), and he started following her. One evening, she phoned me. He was outside the house. Every other time I tried to approach him, he would drive off, so the next time he was watching, I got a couple of friends to block off the road. Well, the strangest thing happened. When I was about to approach him, he must have been having sex in the car with his supposed girlfriend. When he decided to drive off, he was blocked in. When I got to him (you will never believe this), he gets out of the car, no trousers, everything flopping in the wind, and runs up this entry onto the main street. He couldn't face me. He left his car and his half-naked girlfriend. That was the style of the man he was; in fact, he had no style. Suffice to say, we never saw him again. What a stupid bastard.

We made, or should I say she made, a great home for us, and we loved it. It was a top-floor apartment with good views on a clear day; a little small, but it was ours. We had good neighbours and took walks on the beach. It was homely and quite comfortable. She was more relaxed than ever and became her own person, which I believe she liked.

Soon, the inevitable happened. She became pregnant and, unfor-tunately, had a miscarriage, which was really a great loss to us both. Sadness came into our lives for the first time. Unless it has hap-pened to you, it's hard to comprehend. It wasn't too long before she became pregnant again, so we decided to do the honourable thing and get married.

We decided on the registry office in North Shields; family members from both sides attended, except her father. What father does not want to see his daughter happily married? I think it was the word *happily* that bugged him, but he wasn't missed. It was just a small affair, quite funny, really. She was so big, carrying this bundle of joy inside her as the registrar was giving the vows that every time she breathed out (Sandra, that is), she pushed the lectern back. We thought at the time that, being so big, she may be having the pram as well.

The registrar came up to me, asked why we were waiting to go in, and then asked, "Are you sure you want to go through with this?"

I thought, *How strange; ask by all means, but choose a different way.* Sandra was sitting beside me when this question arose, and it upset her, understandably. To try and lighten the mood, I said jokingly, "Have you seen the size of her father?" Well, that didn't really help either.

She delivered my beautiful daughter at ten thirty on the evening of July 17, 1975, not, may I say, without a lot of concerns. She contracted toxaemia and had to be induced at thirty-two weeks, but they were just fabulous, mother and baby. What she went through to get to thirty-two weeks was nothing short of being a bloody miracle, a hero; she was brilliant. I only hope my daughter knows and understands what her mum went through to bring her into this world.

I didn't know you could love something so tiny so much, but we did. The downside was that Sandra suffered from postnatal depression, which, as a husband, is awful to deal with, not to say frightening. I never knew what she was thinking or what pain, mentally, she must have been in. She became distant, wouldn't have anything to do with our baby girl. I often wonder what she was feeling. So it was down to me for the next few months, making sure the baby was fed and clean. She hadn't totally abandoned the baby, but the depression must have been really heartbreaking, and I would go to work worrying. But her mum came and helped tremendously, and she finally overcame this dreadful illness and became a lovely mum, a mum my daughter can be so proud of.

It wasn't long after the birth of Amanda that Sandra fell pregnant again. This was an almighty shock to both of us, as she had contraception fitted in the form of a coil. This was an alternative to having her tubes tied. We thought that, in the future, we may have another child, and this coil would then be removed. But somehow it failed; it split, and so the pregnancy began.

More problems followed. On the first scan, the doctors were saying the wire from the split coil was about to pierce the placenta, and they needed permission to abort the baby. I was adamant that this wasn't going to happen. I would not allow any baby of mine to be aborted. They took me to one side and told me there was a chance the baby would die in the womb or she would miscarry if the placenta was pierced. As the placenta grew, it, in turn, could kill Sandra. This was a no-brainer. She had been through so much; I couldn't take any chances with her life. She found out later, by accident, I think, the baby was delivered alive and a boy, something she always dreamed of. All I could do was cry for her, but leaving this world for the afterlife, we will hopefully be reunited with the child that never was. I don't know whether they christen aborted children. Of course, I never asked.

We moved to Killingworth, where her parents lived, where also they wanted us to be so they could be near Amanda, as neither of them drove. As Sandra wanted to go back to work and we would need a babysitter, it was a logical move but something I was dead against. Where we were, we had fresh air, the beach, great walks, and a lovely environment, but Daddy got his way. He always did with Sandra. Her sister, Linda, was so much more ballsy and headstrong. The move, unfortunately, didn't work out too well. They didn't really want to know, to be honest, and we had moved on a false promise from a beautiful place to an estate that was a nightmare — fights, stabbings, people trying to set the flats on fire. What were we thinking? We just made the best of it till I could find us something more appealing. This wasn't long coming; the council gave us a lovely new house with two bedrooms and a garden in the back on a nice plot.

I guess all this was getting to be too much for us both. I was so unsettled living somewhere I didn't want to be, though grateful I surely was, in a job that was at times life-threatening. Some days I would come home from work as Sandra was leaving the house. I was having panic attacks through lack of sleep and worrying what would happen to them if anything happened to me.

Nobody was bothered about me; at least that's the way I felt. I saw the doctor and he said I was just having panic attacks and to try to stay calm. He gave me some medication, and I took a week's holiday and felt a hell of a lot better after that. With time on my hands, time to think … on reflection, as the breadwinner, I felt I wasn't even in the pecking order at home. My mind started to wander; I was looking for something else. I probably just needed a cuddle, but that wasn't going to happen, and regretfully, I found the cuddle in someone else's arms. That was a massive mistake, but when you're feeling so down and your resistance becomes nonexistent, you become easy prey for other people, and I was.

We sadly parted when my daughter was just over five years old. Her father, my father-in-law, was the cause of most of it, and that's no excuse, but my ex-wife would believe differently. I shed quite a few tears over that and still do even today.

The problem was that he wanted to rule our lives like he ruled his own wife's and children's lives. This was not going to happen. They say blood is thicker than water, and so it proved. We didn't like each other; we just suffered each other for the sake of my daughter, his only grandchild, and peace.

If ever I could have gotten rid of him, I think I would have. In saying that, coming out of the Killingworth Club one evening, he was his usual drunken self. There was snow on the ground and he was sliding everywhere. As we were coming over the bridge, he was being sick. He complained he had lost his false teeth, and believe it or not, he ordered me to hunt for them in the snow. I just helped him over the bridge. He was falling and I couldn't hold him any longer, but I had no intention of stopping him. It wasn't a great fall, but I did my duty and left him there in the snow. He eventually got home. I don't know how, but he did. He never said anything about it. Whether he realised what had happened, I am not sure. I guess we will never know.

I was working at a place called Sterling Organics making drugs (paracetamol) for headaches and anything else you could think of. It was a dangerous place to work, and there were a few deaths involving chemicals the likes of phenol, the elixir of life. Get a couple of inches of that on you, and you'd have about fifteen minutes of life left. I was starting to get panic attacks. It was always, what would happen to my wife and daughter if I was next to die — and I thought I was going to be — but thank God, it passed. The money was good and we could afford to buy our own house, which I was keeping as a surprise. I showed Sandra the house, and she told her father, all excited (Sandra, that is). He told her it was a rope around her neck and to forget about it, which, like an obedient daughter, she did.

It was at this time I started to go off the rails with my family being controlled by a drunk. It was too much for me and it was then I thought, *Shit to this. It's not what I want for my daughter or me.*

I was working in a job where people were dying. I was in a part of the building that was highly dangerous and known for blowing up, so I made plans. I thought, *I will work for myself. I will work the markets, get the products wholesale, and resell them.*

This did not go down well with the family. I mean, there is a pecking order for all of us, but I wasn't even on the bench.

So the markets it was, then. It was great fun, so different and funny. The people you meet on the markets and the clients — I am just surprised how they're all walking round and not locked up — but marketpeople are the salt of the earth, very genuine. I did well, had a few stalls selling perfume, makeup, etc., and that was just to the men. I got involved with clothes, with a wholesaler I became friendly with when I had worked for the stores.

I had decided to leave my wife and child, as there were at least three in my marriage, not including my daughter, whom I dearly love and miss. You will find as this story goes on, when I left, everyone turned against me. I was hated, reviled, and, of course, the opposite was true for my wife. She was held in high esteem and, in a way, quite rightly so. But things with her never sunk in. She could not or did not want to see that her father was the main antagonist.

It's been twenty-two years since I have had contact with my daughter. I write to her four or five times a year, send birthday cards, Christmas cards, and every time, I get no response. Whether, as the mail goes to my ex-wife's address, my daughter gets them or not, I really don't know. She is so filled with hate that I don't exist, and that is so sad. The only time I ever got a reply was from my ex-wife, regarding my will.

Here in Spain it is illegal to disinherit your children unless you can prove they do not wish to be included in any inheritance, or that they have tried to cause harm or murder you. The letter said that if it was my intention to disinherit my daughter, then that was my decision.

I decided I had to send a letter that stated, in English and Spanish, that if it was her wish to have nothing to do with me as a person or with all fiscal matters associated with me, would she be kind enough to sign it and send it back with the stamped, addressed envelope supplied. And the reply was as above. All she said in the letter was that if it was my intention to disinherit her, it was up to me. She also mentioned that she was getting married later that year — my daughter, that is. I assumed September or October, so I responded, "If you need any help, meaning financially, toward the wedding, let me know. It wouldn't be a problem," but I got no response, so back to the story.

The wholesaler and great friend, Florence Cheng, worked out on the islands off Hong Kong, the island of Kowloon. She was a tiny lady, went everywhere with her husband, who never spoke and never smiled. I cannot say with any certainty that he even breathed. He nodded a lot. He was a great nodder. He may have been the business brain, but somehow I don't think so. He may have been better hanging in the back of a car window. She was as smart as a smacked arse and very cute. I asked her to let me know the next time she was visiting England so we could meet up and discuss winter clothing, which always sold well. She did great sweat wear, jeans, cords, cheesecloth shirts, so I was looking to buy the run-offs — when the factories overproduced or there were clothes with slight faults.

Friendly? She was a businesswoman. No such thing as friendly, but we did a bit of business, then the markets started to get taken over by the Indians and Pakistanis. There was no way you could compete with those guys, so it was down to finding a different product. I used to deal with a Jewish guy in Liverpool when I was a bit of a roustabout. I used to deal with him as a mediator for people who were a little bit naughty; you know, like selling their parents' diamonds or jewellery they had borrowed from someone else, probably. Who knows? They came up with the paperwork, which was the most important thing. He would barter rather than buy; you know, this five-speed bike for that diamond bracelet. That sort of thing. Anyway, getting back to selling different products, I thought if anyone had stuff to shift that was different, it would be him; plus, he used to help fund small companies who had cash-flow problems and eventually buy them out, asset-strip, and sell them on.

He liked me and taught me a lot (that's why I have not mentioned his name). He mentored me and helped me become a broker. In fact, as life went on, I became a Master Broker. There were only five in the United Kingdom, and little me was one of them, locally dealing in finance, then on to the markets looking at copper, steel, coffee, arable products. It was an exciting time. I was looking to fund ideas, small companies who found it difficult getting credit because they had no track record. We had the desired credibility and used it to find funding from various quarters: farmers, pension companies, banks, fundholders; companies, for a better word, that we dealt with. We stood as a form of guarantor in return for a percentage of the profits and 51 percent control over all decisions. It became extremely profitable and quite funny.

We decided to back one small company that wanted to sell sex products. They were really profitable. They made jams that you put on parts of your body and that you wanted your partner to lick off, with great names like Rampant Raspberry, Cheeky Chocolate, Orgasmic Orange. They went down a bomb, mainly in the gay community, but it was not easy getting it out into the community. We went to a soft porn channel, which ended up being just hilarious.

CHAPTER 7

Broker Days

The soft porn channel director, who will remain anonymous, was a good man but heavy going. He had the most beautiful woman working for him, as you can imagine, running a soft porn channel. I have never seen as many women with huge busts. There were about six of them (not busts, women) there. I thought, *Fancy getting stuck in a lift with these*, then I thought we wouldn't all fit in the lift. Anyway, I spoke to him regarding advertising this jam product, but he wanted five thousand pounds just to set up the advertising, which was a nonstarter, a definite no-no. The budget we decided that we would work with was not that great. You can only fund so much when there is so little collateral involved. We had to try and make sure our name was on the patent, as some sort of security.

Back to the director. I offered him a percentage of the sales if he agreed the product was feasible. He decided to take it home that evening to try it out. I explained to him it was important the jam was only put on parts he was going to lick or wanted licked off. He said, "No problem," and took the chocolate one.

The following day, I got an irate, angry phone call from what was once my good friend, or associate, anyway. He was absolutely fuming. He called me all the names he could think of, and some of them you couldn't write in this book.

The story goes like this. When he woke up in the morning, he thought someone had crept into his apartment during the night and tarred and feathered him. He was covered in all sorts of shit, from what was in the bed to hair. Even a couple of flies were stuck on his chest. I did explain that I had told him not to cover himself in the jam, just to put it on the parts during sexual foreplay that you want licking off. Did he take my advice? No.

He gets showered and — as he thought he'd gotten most of it, if not all of it, off — he put his shirt on for work. After he had breakfast, he realised that chocolate was seeping through his skin, so, again he showered and changed. On his way to work (he always got the tube), on his way down to the underground at Edgeware Station, he could see people pointing and giggling. Dogs were passing and sniffing at him, and he appeared to be getting a bit of a following. When he turned around, he said, there were about thirty dogs behind him. He said, "I was so angry and looked so foolish. I felt like the Pied Piper of Edgware Road, and these buggers, the dogs that is, must have thought I was a walking chocolate bar."

I asked, "But did it work for you the night before?"

He said, "You cheeky bastard! I will invoice you for all the damage that has been done to clothes, bedding, and reputation."

I said, "That's a shame you didn't listen to me, as it is a very good product, which you have not as yet commented on, which probably means you like it. It's different and if we could put our differences aside, we could make some serious money. This company has also developed condoms that glow in the dark. Would that interest you? And with different flavours."

That calmed him down a bit, and he said, "Maybe. Anything other than that?"

I said, "One company is working on condoms that produce the top ten. The friction starts the music off."

"That's what I want," he said.

"Okay, but let's get these jams organised. An idea, that's what we want. I think the gay clubs; we will present the product as small tins of paint, like the old Airfix kits, selling for around five to ten pounds each."

Without mentioning the club involvement, I must say they went like hotcakes. You wouldn't believe it! Absolutely incredible. So into production we went. It was a crazy time through the clubs and the porn channel. We couldn't produce enough.

The glow-in-the-dark condoms did not take off as we would have liked or expected. It was mainly the kids that bought them. You could see them at night, jeans all aglow, walking round the parks. Quite funny, really. Now, the flavoured ones did well and still are today, but the glow-in-the-dark ones were a total failure. As for the ones that played the top ten, well, they were not exactly something you could play on top of the pops. Sounded more like an octopus being strangled. We lost money on them, but only the pilot costs, so not too bad.

Another good investment was a paint club in Mayfair. She who will be nameless wanted thirty thousand pounds sterling. It was an idea she got from South Africa. The place was small, but had quite plush, thick carpets on the floor. She had a menu of naked women on an easel board; these woman were beautiful, naked, and all over six feet tall, different colours: white, black, brown, yellow … lovely girls, all of them.

The idea was you purchased a really small pot of paint, the girls stood naked in front of you, and the clients (MPs, judges, lawyers, corporate bosses) painted them. There was one very strict rule of no physical or sexual contact. She opened her doors at eleven a.m. and closed at seven p.m. That really was an absolute bonus. The contacts she made were incredible. Did I forget to mention, or have you guessed? She was a top-class madam, charging a minimum of five hundred pounds. She called it corporate bonking. A lovely lady, she had access to all the top events, and I used to get the odd invite.

I liked London and I wanted an office there, so I opened in Cabell Street Marble Arch, close to all the amenities, and I always thought there would be good business in the Arab quarter. I wasn't wrong. They were into property mainly, or anything that made money. The floors of my offices I rented out to other agents looking for accommodation and a London address, a mailbox address, and answering service.

In the meantime, I had divorced my first wife and ended up having a relationship with another lady. She had three lovely children, and my own child seemed to be more distant from me. I put this down to a woman scorned and a family who, whatever I did for them, just hated me. There was never going to be any forgiveness, and this hate, this poison, has spread to my daughter, whom I miss so much. To this day she does not want contact with me, or maybe she does. She surely does not know how hard I have been trying to contact her.

With Amanda, it's possible all the letters and communication are or have been withheld; therefore, she might never know how hard I have tried. Some days this leaves me in turmoil. It's like being in a circle and trying to find a corner to hide in. I have never given up, but there comes a time when it just becomes soul-destroying and affects people around me, so on completion of this book, I will stop looking, writing. But if granted one wish, it would be to see her happy or at least to know she is.

Many years ago, I heard she had a job in Newcastle in Poundland, so I decided to pay her a visit. This didn't exactly go down too well. I saw her serving behind one of the counters and went to say hello, nervous as could be. She just ignored me, and that hurt, but I persevered. She said she didn't want a see me, but by this time, I was wound up and the adrenaline was pumping. I said, "You will see me at lunchtime, or I will come back, put you over my shoulder, kicking and screaming. I will take you out of here."

She agreed. "Come at one o'clock."

This boy rushes out and he was, for some reason, so scared of me that he couldn't get his words out. I didn't realize he came out of the shop. I have never heard anyone stutter so much. I thought he was asking me for money for the bus, so I gave him a pound. Anyway, apparently he was trying to tell me she would be late. I felt a bit bad about that. He must have thought me a crackpot.

Then there she was, simply beautiful. It had been four years since I last saw her. We had some lunch and lots of small talk. We kissed and hugged. There were tears on both sides. I knew then that she still loved me. She went back to work and I offered to take her and her boyfriend (the stutterer who still owes me a pound) for dinner on the Thursday following our lunch. We agreed that I would phone her Wednesday to confirm that everything was okay.

Wednesday came, disaster. Her mother answered the phone and really screamed down the line at me. "You will never see your daughter again. Don't you ever phone this house."

You could have shot me, I was just so devastated. This is how I know or I think she never passed on any of my correspondence; only guilt would make you feel like that. I am convinced that when she told her mum we had seen each other, her mum was frightened in case Amanda asked questions and I told the truth. So I feel her mother has confiscated everything I ever sent for the last twenty-two years: cards, letters, birthday and Christmas cards. I wrote letters but still got no response. I comfort myself with the thought that I have tried, and am convinced when I look back to that phone call that everything sent was kept from her. Even after all this, I always have hope. Hope, they tell me, is the last thing you lose. Maybe there's someone in the great beyond looking down who could help. It's hard to conceive this will be the end of the story, but what else is there? Every time I try, I feel I am hitting a brick wall.

CHAPTER 8

Second Marriage

My second wife, we married after a long courtship of fifteen years. I met her while she worked for Associated Dairies in Newcastle. She was also still married but separated from her husband. She was funny, had a dry sense of humour. Her daughters, three of them, were all different. I remember the youngest coming home just before the summer holidays, asking if she could keep the school's gerbil over the summer holidays, as it was her favourite pet, even to the point of having a gerbil money box. It was at home for about three days and we caught her shaking the life out of the little bugger. She thought it had money inside, just like her gerbil money box. Anyway, it died. I don't know if it was the shaking or when she tried to put a penny up its arse, so we spent a week trying to find something that looked similar to try to replace it.

We decided she needed a pet to look after, so we got her a tortoise as a pet. As kids of five do, for the first week she loved it, taking it up to bed. One night, she was upset. I said, "What's wrong, sweetheart?"

She said, "Will the tortoise die?"

I thought but didn't say, *Not if you try to use it as a money box.* I said, "Eventually, but not for a long, long time, and if it does, we will celebrate its life, have a nice burial, throw a little party for your friends with sweets, jelly cakes, and ice cream."

She said, "Really?"

I said, "Yes."

She said, "Can we kill it now, then?"

Kids.

We decided a new home was on the agenda. She had given up work and the money was coming in, so we moved to the country, Northumberland. We lived in a beautiful place called Bingfield. The property was big, with an inglenook fireplace, and we were really happy there, so we thought we would tie the knot, get married.

So Hexham Registry Office it was, then. We decided after the registry we would go to the church in the village for a blessing. We arrived in the car, stopped outside the church, and nobody — and I mean nobody — was there. We thought we were early and got in the car to tour the village a couple of times. Finally, I said to the driver, "Stop. I will go in and see what's happening." To my surprise, the church was totally empty; even the church mouse had gone. Then we heard singing from the pub across the road, so in I pop to find all my guests and the vicar getting pissed. You couldn't make this up. Eventually we got them out of there, and the vicar was so apologetic I thought, *He will be frightened to charge us after the debacle in the pub.*

Boy, was I wrong! No such luck.

We went through with the blessing and off to the Gosforth Park Hotel for the reception and overnight stay. It was the first hotel I had been in where there was a phone in the toilet. As it was the bridal suite, they offered a choice of beds: king, queen, water. Great hotel, great day, great night.

We decided we would like to move again, into the country, where we were hoping to open a business. It was about this time I decided to have a vasectomy. Well, I didn't decide it, my wife did. How is this for strange: The doctor that did it lived in a place called Long Benton, and he did the procedure in his surgery at New Biggin. I mean, you couldn't make that up.

I shaved myself the night before and had my wicked way. I didn't know how long I would be out of action. Well, that morning, I was a bag of nerves. I went into the surgery, was told to sit, and he then proceeded to make sure I was serious about this procedure. He prepared his tools for the job, and give him his due, he did try to talk me out of it for a fee.

I could hear him behind me, testing his little circular saw (really) and stuff; then he got this syringe. I have never seen anything so big. I thought, *I bet he thinks I have come here for artificial insemination.* I lifted my arm up for the jab, but he went straight between my legs. I was paralysed. My arm stayed in that position throughout the operation, my face looking straight ahead. I was in shock. He cut open my testicles (I know you don't want to hear this, but you're going to), tied my tubes, sewed me back up, and told me to go home, which I gladly did.

That night, I couldn't sleep. It was always there in the morning to say hello to me and slap my wife on the bum, so I waited and waited. Then, there it was, raising its little head. I thought, *You beauty, you'll be okay.* The other good thing was that it was black. I thought, *Ah, the icing on the cake.* Would I do it again? Of course I wouldn't.

We moved house and rented on the golf course for a while, waiting for our purchase of the tearooms in the Lake District in Allendale to complete. It still needed work done on it, and was not really ready for occupation, plus the kids needed to move schools.

The house we rented must have been built by Lego, or what they had left over. It was close to the golf course, but nothing worked as it should. We had floods, fire, pestilence, and neighbours straight out of the 1920s, or that's how they seemed — certainly how they dressed. We had floods like you could never believe.

One evening, I was holding the ceiling up, water pouring through. The dog, we had a sheep dog, was pawing at the gas and electric box. All of sudden, an explosion blew me across the floor and sent the dog flying through the air into next door's lounge. I was black and blue, not to mention singed; the dog was bald; and the neighbours were looking through the hole the dog created, saying, and I quote, "Our television has gone off," unquote. After we put the fire out and drained the place of water, we decided enough was enough; we would live in the tearooms as they were.

Allendale, now there was a strange place. You always felt that in the olden days it had a dark side to it. It was quite famous for its tar barrels and bonfires at New Year, stretching back to the Viking invasion. The bonfires were to warn villages along the coast that they were under attack from invaders, but the locals, if you could have seen them, would have looked more at home in Sherwood Forest. It wasn't that they were slow or backward; they were stuck in a time warp. If we ever get invaded from outer space, let's hope they go there first. That way, they may think they should give this planet a miss. I can say this: They would be made welcome. The tearoom was situated in a large square or plaza, had seven pubs, well, six. One was temperance, no booze allowed.

The tar barrels. The men wore these on their heads so it was easier for the Vikings to see and shoot them, I suppose. Didn't I say it was a strange place? I will never forget the day we moved in. Nearly seven hours, it took us. I was in the bath getting clean, you know, ear, nose, and throat, and I have to say the banister got a good clean as well before I got out of the bath. There was a knock on the door and my good wife answered it, thinking it was a kindly neighbour.

Well, it turned out to be the monster of the village, selling apples. It looked like he had caught fire and someone tried to put him out with a baseball bat. I ask you, at eight thirty in the evening? It was a bag full of apples, and I have to admit it frightened her to a degree. It cost her fifty pence. When I looked in the bag, they were all rotten, so I grabbed the bag, opened the door, and she said, "Please don't do anything. We're new here."

I said, "We are new here, but we're not stupid here," so I rushed out, just a towel around my waist, shouting at this bloke. I said, "Hey, you thieving bastard, get back here."

He looked at me, and I am no slouch: six foot tall, broad shoulders. He must have thought, *Shit*. Well, he started to run, so I chased him across the plaza with just my towel on, throwing the apples after him. The neighbours must have thought, *Goodness me, what's arrived?*

He ran through a copse. I wasn't going in there, but shouted, "We will meet again."

Next day, he comes in the shop (which we were knocking into shape) with his sister, and he apologised. I realised then he wasn't exactly all there, so I felt a bit bad as well, but it was dark and we were tired, and if the truth is known, I was hoping to have sex in my new house, so that put the kybosh on that. He turned out to have a good heart, as did most of the neighbours, when they realized we were quite normal. I mean, the kids were not, but we were.

We decided to keep the tearooms and do afternoon teas and sandwiches, cakes, bread, etc.; meals in the evening; Sunday lunches; etc. We thought it may be a good idea to use three of the bedrooms as a bed and breakfast, and it's fair to say we were quite busy and, in our own little way, successful. We had John, a typical local, the man I had chased across the square trying desperately to choke him on his apples; but you know, he was a good soul.

His sister used to phone and apologise about sending him messages. He would walk into the shop, a fag in his mouth, a French beret just sitting on his head, coughing (he stunk of smoke), and wearing a coat straight out of the 1920s that would have looked more at home on a camel. You would need a wok to iron it and get the lumps and bumps out, but this is typical John.

He walks in the shop, admires himself in the mirror for about five minutes; then he starts. "I need a loaf."

"Okay, large or small?"

He thinks. "Large."

"Square or round?"

He thinks again. "Square."

"Brown or white?"

He thinks. "Brown."

"Cut or uncut?"

He now is totally thrown and I have spent five minutes with him. He says, "Can I phone my sister?"

I said, "Yes, what's the number?"

He said, "One, two, three," so, like an idiot, I started to dial.

I thought, *He is getting to me*, so I eventually get the correct phone number.

He says on the phone to her, "Cut or uncut?"

She says, "John, it's a custard you've gone for."

On reflection, funny as hell, but a genuine bloke. At New Year, they had people from all over the world come and watch the tar barrels. There was a huge bonfire in the middle of the square; the townspeople circled the fire with these barrels spitting out fire on their heads. There was live music, jazz bands playing in the four quarters of the square, all the pubs — seven of them — all open, people's doors open. Drinks flowed freely. It was quite amazing. We had people on the floor sleeping in the shop. Just a fabulous night. We did hot dogs, and I have to say, we made a few bob.

The tearooms were great, but running two jobs was just too much. I decided I needed a year off from the brokerage, anyway, just to recharge my batteries, so I did some work at the local dairies and spent a year helping with children at Pendower Special School, chauffeuring them back and forth.

What brave, courageous children they were. Their bones were all twisted and they had so many problems, twisted in all sort of shapes, but a smile for everyone. They always had time for each other and all those around them, even with all their disabilities. They loved people, and believe it or not, they loved life. They invited me to an end-of-school disco they were having, all their own work. The way they dressed the hall, the music they chose — it was just incredible. They would approach each other as the music was playing, ask each other to dance, and move their bodies, while still in their wheelchairs, to the music. What a tearjerker. Incredible people with incredible teachers and incredible views of life, while suffering with enormous physiological problems.

I looked after three children there. Simon was autistic. Sarah suffered from multiple sclerosis; though she was in a wheelchair, she wore callipers, and lifting her in and out! Goodness me, I ended up with muscles in my spit. And there was David, who had brain dysfunctions. He boarded at a local school and was away all week. I used to take him on a Monday and pick him up on a Friday. He was a lovely boy, and could he swear! He could teach me a few things, but his parents must have found it extremely difficult to manage him at home all week.

Once, a police car passed us on the way home. David, only about eight, started giving the officers the "V" sign, so they pulled me over.

Then came the questions. "Do you know what your son is doing in the back of your car, sir?"

I said, "No, but before you start, two things. One, he isn't my son, and two, I didn't see anything."

The officer shouted in to David, "Is this your father?" to which David replied, "Yes, it is." Did that take some explaining!

Sarah, sadly, died after I left. Such a lovely child. She only spoke well of everyone; she was magical. I often think back to her, but if there is a God in Heaven, she will be quite close to him, giving him advice as she gave me — an angel, indeed. I'm not sure who is the lucky one.

Simon was autistic. He used to tell he was going trespassing during the weekend. I said, "Trespassing where?"

He said, "Social Security."

They had offices in a square with a board that said "No Trespassing." He thought it was brilliant. I used to take the rise out of them all on different days and we used to laugh at each other, but what fun he was! They all were. His parents let him watch the most violent movies till three in the morning. By the time I collected him, he was sleepwalking. You couldn't help but love them, and, you know, that's all they wanted. They had so much to give, and were grateful for what they had. We should step back and look in the mirror and thank God we are what we are. These kids can teach us so much.

Pendower was something I was pleased to have done. It brings you down to Earth and makes you feel so grateful that you and your children are in good health. I believe everyone should have that experience; then maybe people would be grateful for what they have, maybe even help the needy, the people who have very little in life who are stuck in a bubble, looking for a way forward. So, thank you, Pendower, for all the wonderful work you are doing and for making me a better person in the process.

It was about this time my father died. We don't really know what the cause was. We assumed it was old age combined with diabetes, but he suffered in silence; he wasn't one to be fussed over.

I can remember getting to the hospital and seeing my mother holding my dad's hand. He appeared to be in the foetal position, all curled up. My mother's last words to him were quite simple: "Where have you hidden your money, Harold?"

My dad, with a wry smile on his face, whispered, "Somewhere you'll never find it."

He died not long after. It was around eighteen months later that my mum died. We think it was pneumonia. The hospital staff were quite vague, to be honest. When my brother and I were clearing the house, we found Dad's money hidden in a pile of ironing. My mother hated ironing and it was a no-go area in our house, so he hid his money there. Clever sod.

I had great parents and was so lucky. One of the last things we did was take Mum to my niece's, her granddaughter's, wedding. She married a Greek guy. The wedding was so expensive, we paid for the flowers and the buttonholes. We paid to enter the church, we paid to get out, and we paid at the reception. The reception was good, though. There was wine and whisky and beer on everyone's table, and when they were up dancing, my mother decided to collect the whisky bottles and put them in her bag, which, by the way, was no ordinary bag. This could carry a week's shopping, so at the end of the evening, my mother refused to leave, saying she couldn't move her legs, owing to the fact she couldn't get off the chair she was on. I think all the whisky she consumed had weighed her down, so my brother and I carried her out on the chair, a bit like the pope, then went back for her bag. Trust me, you couldn't lift it. It took two of us to take it to the car, which looked suspicious, to say the least, not to mention the bottles rattling. We heard through the grapevine that they were pleased with the reception, but they went through some whisky.

It was decision time. My wife wanted to move. Being out in the country is a nice thing, but not if you're a city-dweller, and she was a city person. We decided to invest in a new house in Four Stones, a small village just outside Hexham. We had it built, and it turned out to be a lovely estate, but to pay for it, it was back to work — back to being a broker.

We had a good reputation and knew the right people, so I started making a few phone calls, opened an office in London, then got a contract to find land and grants for building contractors to invest in France. It was mainly lake and coastal land they were looking for, preferably within twenty-five miles of Paris, but there were lovely sites becoming available in Valenciens and San Salve, which was more north. But government grants were plentiful. An added advantage was a girl from Durham, not far from where we lived in the North East, was married to the local mayor, which would prove to be a great help.

Discussions with the local mayors were never easy. Their town or village would have to prosper, you can make your mind up about that. We needed their approval, which was forthcoming, depending on the amount of employment we could bring to the area. This, of course, was also lots of brownie points for them on the political front and securing future employment as mayor. With their agreement, the next job was finding out what grants may be available, then on to the banks to see what they would offer, then to the tax offices to see what we might get in tax-free encouragements in the form of delayed or reduced payments. I have to say I met some lovely people, but each one was hard work.

It was at this time I had an office on Cabal Street in London, and rented office space, as I thought, to two nice girls from Devon who were doing, as they had told me, interior design. Well, if you lived in London and didn't have your own interior designer, you were a nobody.

Anyway, I digress. I was working late one night, and just along the hallway by the toilets, we had a kitchen for coffee, etc. As I say, I was working late one night and my mind must have been somewhere else. I come out of the kitchen, coffee in hand, and this guy, totally naked, walks out of the toilet. He sees me and screams. Well, I scream back. The next thing I know, he takes off down the corridor, the cheeks of his arse going up and down like giant saddlebags, straight into one of the girls' rooms. The interior designer, her name was Hazel. The next thing I knew, there was knock on the door; it was Hazel.

"Noel," she cried out. "Can I have a word?"

I said, "No, Haze. I am busy, and for the record, I didn't see anything." I was thinking she may be having an affair, and I didn't want to get involved, but her pleas continued, so I let her in.

She explained straight out of the blue that they were not interior designers but sexual consultants. I didn't know what to think or say;

I didn't even understand what that was. All sorts of connotations were going through my mind. Was I fronting a brothel? I was gob-smacked.

I said, "I have just given you the opportunity to say nothing to get out of this. You didn't have to tell me. Why?"

She said, "Don't be annoyed, but he wants you to watch."

I said, "What?"

She said, "He wants you to watch."

I said, "You're kidding."

She said, "No, there is twenty pounds in it for you."

I said, "Really? What do I do?"

She said, "Just sit and watch."

I said, "For how long?"

She said, "A few minutes."

Curiosity overcame me, along with the thought of twenty pounds, of course. So I go in and he is lying there on the bed, not a stitch on, but with his penis erect. Not quite erect — it sort of veered off to the left.

He said to me, "What do you think?"

My first thought was, *Shoot him.* My second one was, *Twenty pounds.* I said, "Super."

She said a few erotic words to him, like, "I am going to rip your scrotum off and shove it up your arse" (and I bet she could have). With those gentle words, he arrives, and comes with a whimper.

I thought, *Amazing. Three minutes, twenty pounds.*

When he left, we had a chat. She told me he was there three times a week, so I said, "Book me in, and just for the record, what's a sex consultant?"

She said, "Around fifty pounds for fifteen minutes."

I thought, *Jesus! I am in the wrong job.* "What's his job?" I asked.

"He works for the local council as a parking inspector," she said.

She charged him fifty quid a time; to anyone else, she would offer a discount. I am thinking my flight from Newcastle to London return was forty-five pounds. That would do for me.

She said she and her friend put on a lesbian act for a washing-machine millionaire (who will be nameless) every second Tuesday of the month, and they usually needed a hand to put up the parachute.

I said, "Parachute?"

She said, "Yes, we hang it from the ceiling and make the place look like an Arab's tent, cushions all over the floor and a comfy chair for him to watch the action in."

I said, "Comfy chair?"

She said, "Yes, he is in his seventies but believes he is a young buck. We get three empty bottles of champagne, one full one, and open the full one when he arrives. He always has a couple of whiskies before a glass of champagne with the girls. We put an aspirin or paracetemol in his drink, and he is fast asleep in about five minutes. We have a bit of a fumble, open the poor bugger's trousers; he wakes up, thinks he has seen a great show and drank three bottles of champagne. He calls for his chauffeur, parts with a thousand pounds, and goes home a very happy customer."

I had an opportunity to work for a large accounting firm just outside London, dealing with repossessed property, goods, shops, everything. My main job was to organise property sales out of auction. These were houses that would go to auction for sale to the highest bidder, and usually went for a song. It was my job to get rid of them before the auction happened.

I could see this was going to be quite lucrative, so we moved out of London to deal with property mainly in the Finchley area. I had an offer from two investors there to organise sales and finance in the housing boom, so everything was slipping into place. The directors were two gay girls, and they offered me accommodation in their plush apartment building. Nothing ever happened. They just viewed me as a big brother. Though they had nothing to do with men, they used to buy each other X-rated porn videos as birthday and Christmas presents. They just wanted my knowledge and input about the property market, which at that time was not so limited, to say the least, and mainly to put deals together that were suitable to the banks and for the buyers.

The banks were a pushover. I had dealt with them for years. Most of the managers in London, our capital city, were spineless and could not make decisions or were frightened to do so, unlike the North East, where you could have an agreement up to 250,000 pounds. Of course, London properties were so much more expensive, but volatile. Almost everyone in banking there was terrified; make a wrong decision and your bonus was gone. We all know what bankers' bonuses are like, don't we? But the property market has always been a boom-and-bust market in the south, so decisions made had to be 100 percent correct.

We were quite successful. We made some good money. We were, or I was, getting business from people like Price Waterhouse, defunct businesses and property repossessions, working out subsidy schemes for potential customers and making the properties look inviting. Of course we were making money in the bargain — not megabucks, but a living.

I moved to Braintree in Essex and worked with my late accountant there, selling houses and brokering business. He was a really funny man. He was the image of Charlie Drake, the comedian. He was a generous man for an accountant. We worked all over Essex. I then had a contract offer from one of England's big builders. The referral came from the lady for whom I raised the money for the paint club in London. He was a director and apparently a good customer of hers. We had always kept in touch (my lady friend, that is), and if there were anything good coming up, like a box at Ascot for the races or seats at Silverstone for the Grand Prix, we would try to attend. She was into everything, and who she didn't know just wasn't worth knowing.

So my services were acquired for buying land in France, as I have previously mentioned, preferably coastal or large lake land. It was my job to track down the opportunities, speak to the owners, speak to the local mayor and banks. It was a twelve-month contract that paid extremely well. In saying that, they still owe me three thousand pounds, which, of course, I will never see. Their criterion was always the same: find me land within twenty-five miles of Paris. It would have been easier to have had an audience with the pope, but we managed, just.

At the end of the contract, I went back to Essex, bought a house, and ran my brokerage from there. Houses there were not cheap, but the place I fancied was in Coggleshall, a nice village famous for being haunted. A ghostly community. This house came up for sale, and when I asked the people why they were selling, they were quite honest and said, "It's haunted and we're going. We would like to sell as soon as possible. All sensible offers would be considered."

This just appealed to me. It had about a quarter of an acre, maybe a tad more, with it, and pets: two chickens, which I named Sam and Ella. They were lovely pets and very clever. I got eggs from them on a regular basis and really took to them.

In the summer, at lunchtime, I would get out a deck chair to catch some sun, have a sandwich and a glass of wine. It was really peaceful, and the chickens would sit on the top of the chair on either side of my head. In the morning, they would tap on the French windows, come into the kitchen, up onto the draining board, and tap on the cupboard above. That's where I kept their corn. They really were amazing. When Ella wanted to go to the toilet, Sam would dig a hole for her, and when she had finished, he'd fill it in. They say animals are dumb, but far from it. The only problem I had was the postman. They would attack him for some reason. I don't know why; he was always nice to them. I can only think he had bills in his hand for me. Now that's loyalty for you.

When I first moved in, I got friendly with the farmhand who worked next door. He was a real grafter; lovely lad, wife, two kids.

Since the farm ran toward and alongside my land with just a wire fence between us, we always had time for a chat. He was telling me that this was his last week and after that he had no job, and asked did I know of anything going. I said sorry. Then he told me the wages were a pittance, anyway. I said I was looking for more land and asked if he'd like to earn some extra cash. He agreed.

I said, "If I get a digger in, can I take twenty-five to thirty feet of your land? All you have to do is take the fencing down and put it up again twenty-five feet nearer."

He said the farmer was on holiday so we would have to be quick. With that, we got to work and I extended my property by 375 square feet. Now, that's what I called a result. I thought, *I have just created a nice client car park and possibly, with the council's permission, a site for a new office.*

I employed a fabulous lady who once worked for my accountant. She was very smart, very clever, and we became great pals, soul mates. Nothing funny. She was married to her husband, Rob, whom she adored, but we were great mates. We could have been brother and sister. We were very close. We went back across the channel to see what business we could drum up there in the form of properties and businesses for sale, and we took our less-than-seaworthy accountant, who was terrified of water.

I told him, "Thirty-five minutes on the hovercraft and you're there."

He said he had heard it was over three hours.

I said, "Maybe on the boat, but this is the hovercraft. It's much quicker."

Anyway, to cut a long story short, he spent the whole time in the toilet, and when we landed thirty-five minutes later, he was still in the toilet. I told him we had landed, but he just didn't believe me. It took us and the cabin crew nearly another fifteen minutes to convince him and get him out. What a pain in the arse. The captain threatened to call the police; otherwise he would still be in there today.

People were moving to France to start a new life, young couples especially. With good food and cheap housing, it was so easy at the end of your working week to jump on a hovercraft, and you were there in thirty-five minutes. We went down to northern France to a place called La Touquet. This was the French Riviera of the north, and we collaborated with a few agents and started advertising cheap trips to show the available properties. We also had a round house that was built for a film in the Valley de Course. Everything in it was round, designed by the late Bridget Bardot's husband, Roger Vandim. A fantastic property, it had a river than ran across the bottom, full of trout. There were so many, you could talk them out of the river. It really looked like something special when the whole place was lit up in the evening, like a film set, which is what it originally was.

I used to go home to Hexham every two weeks. I always had a week at home to spend time with the kids and my wife. The kids were going through a strange phase. Sarah attempted suicide over a dog she had found. I said she couldn't keep it, that someone would be missing it, but there was no way to pacify her, so she said she was going to kill herself.

Trying to help, I said, "Can you do it quietly?"

The next thing I know, I find out my bottle of gin is gone and my razor is missing. I tell my wife, who says, "What would she want the gin and razor for?"

I said, "Maybe she wants to shave the dog but needs to get it drunk first."

She replied, "Oh."

A couple of hours later, she came back in, looking the worse for wear, and threw up on the cat, which shocked and annoyed me. I didn't know we had a cat. But in general, as kids go, they were pretty good.

I could have only been home a few weeks after five years in the south and disaster happened. We had major problems with our bank, the Bank of Credit and Commerce. It closed its doors after being accused of money laundering. I say accused. It actually was money laundering. Everyone lost money; even councils lost millions. It was the most terrible decision never thought out, just a knee-jerk reaction by the Yanks.

We, like numerous companies, were not protected by the financial services or the government. They just didn't care that companies were going to the wall. We went bankrupt. Two weeks prior to all this happening, we had bought new cars — leased, of course. The leasing company wanted their money, not the cars back. It was horrendous; I had to go before various committees, the Securities and Investment Board, the FSA as it is now. They were looking for scapegoats and, as usual, looking in the wrong place. They didn't realise thousands of people were affected, or maybe they did. We had no access to anything — large companies, councils. One particular council in Scotland lost thirteen million pounds. We all banked with them, as their interest rates were so good.

So, it was the Social Security for me for the very first time, and time to take stock of what to do. We had mortgages, all sorts of bills to pay, and nothing to pay them with.

Being interviewed by Social Security for benefits, something I had never claimed, was most unusual. It was worse than the Spanish Inquisition. They wanted to know everything about me. This lasted for about twenty-five minutes. For the life of me, I swear that they do not listen to what you say. They are just looking for an excuse to pay you as little as possible, or nothing at all, asking me why I thought I was a deserving case for benefits after their bosses. The government was the cause of the problems in the first place.

I told them it was people like me keeping people like them in a job. I said, "There are four of you here. I guess, between you, your earnings are about eighteen thousand pounds a year. Last year, I paid 21,640 pounds in tax, so if you like, I paid all your salaries and more."

The most stupid replied, "You must have earned a lot of money."
I said, "I did."

"Well, where is it and what are you doing here?"

I said, "It's in the Bank of Credit and Commerce that your bosses, the government, shut down — closed, without prior notice or warning to anyone — and that is, in the meantime, landing me in front of you. Do you people not understand that the actions the government has taken will destroy people's lives, and without a care in the world, not knowing the damage they were creating without thought. And these politicians, who probably had their money invested, you can bet your life they were not affected. With a motto in these we trust, not likely," I said. "The one good thing to come out of this is that your jobs are safe."

"Really?" was the reply.

I said, "Yes, they are, as you're going to get really busy all of a sudden."

I was informed by the lady on the inquiry panel, "We will let you know." She never said much but had that look like it was that time of the month, very pit bullish, and the only difference between her monthly cycle and a pit bull was the lipstick. "But we will suspend your benefits for six weeks," she said.

I asked, "How can you suspend something you have never given or offered me?"

The reply was, "This interview is over."

So I asked the most stupid question. "If I find a part-time job for six weeks, will this affect my benefits, assuming you will offer me something?"

They said, "Yes, you won't get any."

"Well, how do I live?"

The answer was a shrug of the shoulders.

So I went taxiing at night around the clubs with my car, and on Sundays did the markets with my brother. I didn't earn a fortune but put food on the table and managed to pay a couple of bills. I had to be careful. My mortgage was 1,332 pounds a month, 333 pounds a week that they were obliged to pay; consequently, they had me followed everywhere I went, trying to catch me working so they could suspend my benefits. Of course, apart from the taxiing and markets, I was a good boy. I felt sorry for the guy that was tailing me, especially here in a North East winter, sitting in a car with about three feet of snow around him. The poor bugger must have been frozen.

It's funny. I said to my wife, "Let's take him out a cup of tea," which I did at first.

He pretended he didn't know who I was, but he relented and he was grateful. A bacon sandwich, and we were friends for life. It got to the stage where he and I were watching morning TV together. He hated his job, but, as he said, they needed to catch me working so they could stop any and all benefits. I don't think he ever realised the only reason they sent him to watch me was to get him out of the way. An important member of staff would never be sent. I guess it just went straight over his head.

Winter had come and gone. There was no news from the bank regarding the savings we had in Credit and Commerce, so a bank manager friend of mine whom I used to do a lot of business with, and who had good holidays on the business I brought in, offered to fund a venture for me. Back into the mortgage business I was, so I opened a small shop in Whitley Bay and started again. It was slow at first, but picked up. I managed to employ an ex-con (didn't know that at the time) who worked for the Social Security Pension Department in Newcastle.

Well, he once did. They gave him the job of plugging holes where people were claiming pensions they were not entitled to, or where the intended recipients were dead. He realised how profitable it was and decided that he would claim the dead ones' on their behalf. He had 2,200 pounds salted away and never spent a penny of it in case he got caught, which he eventually did. He gave all the money back and got sentenced to two years in prison, which he thought was a bit harsh. But you steal from the government, and you pay.

He had a good heart and just wanted to work. He was honest with me, so I took a chance and it turned out to be a good move. We became good friends, and to this day, we still are, but did he have some baggage or what! A wife who had five kids with four different partners, and who was having sex with the guy next door while he was at work.

I said to him, "Do something about it."

"What about the kids?"

I said, "What do you do while your wife is having sex in the next room?"

He said, "Listen. It turns me on."

I asked, "What does your wife say?"

He said, "She doesn't know I am there."

I think that was the only strange thing about him. I mean, no man in his right mind would listen to his wife having sex with another man unless it was a huge turn-on or she was getting paid for it. I thought, *For all I know you, I don't really know you at all.*

Business was good. We had some great clients. I applied for my credit license back, went before the Securities and Investment Board while supported by the Office of Fair Trading, which resurrected my broker status. I got my license back from the Office of Fair Trading and started again.

I thought we might delve into different ventures. Getting back into the banks because of the bankruptcy was proving difficult. The building societies were not as strict. They just wanted business and proof you were licensed to do it, so I decided to take on the task of repossessions and refinancing trade agreements with loan companies.

Because of all the new laws that were coming in, it was difficult, but if people had problems, they would rather talk to me than their bank or building society manager, so we approached various companies as problem solvers. We only got paid if we solved the problem, so this appealed to most companies. They liked this idea. To them, what harm could it cause? To a degree, it was free.

We were inundated with business in as much as there were so many people out there not knowing which way to turn, struggling to get out of the messes they were finding themselves in. They had little faith in the Citizens Advice Bureau, and people were advised to seek us out. We were quite successful in that we helped solve about 20 percent of the problems, which under the circumstances might not seem a lot, but there were some problems that were unsolvable. It also helped that I had an old lawyer friend who sadly went off the rails a bit when his wife divorced him. He was more than glad to help, plus it was extra revenue for him, which he dearly needed, as he was more or less unemployable. Plus he was a friend and he knew I would be keeping an eye on him. So there's me, an ex-bankrupt, an ex-con, and an unemployable solicitor. What a crew! But together, we were formidable.

I cannot say we broke eggs with a big stick, but we did make, as I say, some progress. We made some people's lives that bit better, but didn't earn a lot of money. I mean, the yacht I was considering buying was getting smaller by the day. In saying that, rowing is good for your muscles and your paunch, but not the seagoing adventure I was looking for. Ah, well, there's still the lottery.

The funny thing about the lottery. If I am lucky enough to win it, I will probably be in a vegetive state and won't understand it anyway. Isn't it funny that the people who win don't need it (the millionaires of this world), or are the rogues of society who don't deserve it, and it's never, as they say, going to change their lives. There they are, making this statement, standing by their Rolls-Royce in the harbour of Monaco with a bottle of Guinness in their hands and a bag of crisps. I wonder if they think the bag of crisps still makes them working class. There surely is nothing queerer than folk.

CHAPTER 9

New Start

The office in Whitley Bay was doing okay, and we had a good name amongst the locals because we were there; not a soft touch, but a shoulder to cry on. We never stood in judgement on anyone. Everyone is entitled to make a mistake. As I grow older, I have learned that pleasing everyone is impossible, but pissing them off is a piece of cake. In saying that, as you grow older, there are mistakes and mistakes, and rectifying them doesn't come easy. But we've all been there and, for sure, none of us are perfect. But we had a philosophy of treating people like we would want to be treated. We always believed that arrogance breeds contempt and humility breeds friendship. This worked for us. We gained people's trust and their business.

It was about this time that I had a wandering eye. I was getting more unsettled at home. I don't know why; my wife and I had a pretty good relationship. We had been together for fifteen years, and it wasn't a case of the grass being greener on the other side, because it never is. I was my wife's third husband and there were three children, two from previous husbands. She had two with her first: Deborah and Sarah. She had two more with the second: John Paul and Laura. Unfortunately, the first one, John Paul, died. Her first husband, Robert, for sure was her greatest love.

I am not the sort of person who competes with other people's ex-husbands. I don't think you can. What you can do is offer some-thing different. In this case, it was humour. She loved my sense of humour; so did the kids. I could make them laugh. The hard part was that they always felt a sense of loyalty to the husband before, which is understandable. But they grew to love me, never knowing what to expect.

In return, I gave them a sense of humour. I taught them to laugh at adversity, to laugh at themselves, to be respectful, to love each other, to be there for each other. When I arrived, there were con-stant battles in their lives. I taught them to listen to each other in an argument instead of shouting over each other, and when we had the tearooms, I taught them how to earn tips, extra cash from the customers, and to dress properly.

Sometimes they would come down with so much metal attached to their faces you would have thought they had fallen into some-body's tackle box. I mean, Christmas presents were easy: a tin of metal polish and a tube of Super Glue and they were made up. When they took off all the metal, they had more holes in their faces than the Wentworth golf course. It was on their faces, noses, ears, and eyebrows. You could imagine it was like talking to a piece of Gouda cheese. But they had good hearts. They may never be aca-demic, but they had the most important trait, common sense, and they were polite. You could take them anywhere. Couldn't leave them, but could take them anywhere.

My solicitor's secretary, the very lovely Meg, was to be my third wife. I have never met someone with such a good heart. We had met early on in life, when my divorce from my first wife was being finalized. I tried then to convince her to ditch the unhappy mar-riage she'd found herself in with her husband. He was not only a bully, but a coward as well. He was okay abusing women, a real tough guy, but when it came to men, he was a coward; no balls whatsoever. Alas, she decided to stay with the lunatic and his family (he had been married before), but thankfully, she had no children with him.

Life drifted on for me until I started trading again in Whitley Bay. I needed a solicitor for the shop lease and future clients. When dealing with people and professionals, you needed people around you who you were confident in and comfortable with. Alan, my solicitor, was brilliant — not cheap, but in life, you get what you pay for. He was honest and a real safe pair of hands.

Meeting Meg for the second time was amazing, and she was still working for him. She didn't look too good, so I invited her for a coffee. She told me then about her crap husband and the sadness in her life.

Meg. It was sad, really. She worked hard for the company. There is nothing she wouldn't do for anybody or help with, and people really did take advantage. She worked for the company for twenty-five years before they made her redundant. Their excuse was that her position was made redundant. What price, loyalty?

I said, "Come and work with me," which she did. She finally left her husband, and he was quite upset about it, but on reflection, I don't believe he loved her. It was his pride he was worried about, when everyone would find out she had dumped him.

We got closer. She found a flat and I used to visit. Things really got serious between us, and finally, I left home to move in with her.

Her husband decided to have her followed. He had heard she was seeing someone from the shop in Whitley Bay, but every time he passed the shop, I was never there. My colleague, Brian, was. Him being five foot two and portly, he must have been shocked that she would fall for someone, let's say, so different from him. He was more tall and skinny.

It was about this time that Brian began to behave quite strangely. I asked what the problem was and he said, "If I tell you, promise you won't laugh."

I said, "I promise."

"I think I am being stalked. I know I am being followed."

Well, I had to break my promise, and I laughed. I asked, "With respect, who would want to stalk or follow you?"

He said, "Every morning, I get out of the shower, stand in front of the mirror naked, and ask myself the same question. 'Who would want to follow me?'"

You can imagine — we just couldn't think who it might be, so the thick plottons or is it the plot thickens? Then one day I was behind my car with the boot open and my name was called out. I said, "That's me," and as I closed the boot, the guy got a bit of a shock.

He said, "Is that you?"

I said it was. Well, here is the rub. I am six feet tall and broad, muscles in my spit, not the five-foot-two, portly guy he had been following. Yes, it was him. To Brian's relief, I let him know that the fool thought he was me. He told me his name; it was Meg's husband. He all of a sudden was gobsmacked and short of words.

I said, "Oh, yes. I have heard about you. You like frightening women, don't you? Do you fancy trying to frighten me?"

He said, "Do you know my family?" They were known for being a bit nasty.

I told him, "You want to go to war with me, you'll never leave this pavement." I told him, "You ever lay a hand on her and I will lay more than a hand on you." I said, "You don't scare me, and your family certainly doesn't bother me, not if you're a prime example."

So, I told her, and in all fairness, she was frightened, but he was an arsehole. The only tough thing about him was the boots he was wearing. Anyway, we settled down and there were no more problems, although he did try to follow me, always on the weekends. Not him, but two guys.

Now, I belong to a family that once controlled a city, and I made a couple of phone calls and had some friends come up. As usual, the weekend came round, and again, they were following me, but this time I had help. I drove up a blind alley, and they followed, as did my friends. We blocked the car in and dragged them out of it. You could smell the adrenalin. In fact, you could see it running down their legs. They were petrified, so they went back and told the husband they didn't want to get involved, and that was the last of that.

We bought a house close to the sea, well, Whitley Bay was on the coast, and started fresh. We had a great thing for each other, and in seventeen years, it's gotten even better. I chose Whitley Bay, as that's where I was when Amanda had been born twenty-three years earlier, and there is something about the coast and the people. It was like North Shields, an old fishing village.

I remember a shop called Pantrini's, a family-run fish-and-chip shop. The food was superb, as was the family. The matriarch, Babs, ran the show. You could go down there during teatime on a Friday — well, any day of the week, come to mention it — and you'd be treated like one of the family. You would order your fish and chips, and while you were waiting, she would serve you black Russians. This was a drink with Coca-Cola plus Tia Maria plus vodka. Fantastic! Not many fish-and-chip shops offer that while you're waiting. By the time you downed three or four of them, you often went home without the fish and chips you had originally come for. Beautiful people.

Business was good, but I was in need of change — getting restless — so I said, "Let's move to Spain." I had done a few jobs over there for clients in different parts of the country — finance, etc. — and really fancied the move. As we were both in agreement, we started to make plans. I went to night school to start to learn the language.

The only thing we were not in agreement on was the house. She wanted to rent the house. I disagreed. I said, "If we're going, let's sell; burn our bridges, sell the house. That way, the effort we make over there to earn a living will be more intense." We finally agreed. She put her trust in me, and I have never let her down.

CHAPTER 10

Life in the Costas

We had a great going-away party, and the usual sceptics said it wouldn't last a month (seventeen years later, we are still here). Don't you find it amazing that people you invite — friends, family, and so forth — to a nice party, who you water and feed at your own expense, wouldn't at least wish you good luck for the future, even if they didn't mean it? The old saying, "There's nothing funnier than folk," really does ring true.

Leaving was quite dramatic. The plane we were to leave on had problems and was grounded, so it was a long wait till a replacement arrived, and when it did, it looked like something the Wright brothers had just created. It was frightening. It appeared as if it had been in a crash and glued back together. I have never seen anything so old. The interior, to say the least, was wrecked.

Once on the plane, we were told by the air hostess to sit anywhere we liked. The food was a can of pop and a packet of crisps; the cabin crew looked like they hadn't shaved in months, and that was just the trolley dollies. When the captain arrived, he looked like he would have been more at home driving a bus than a plane.

We made about three attempts to take off. I can only assume he had trouble with the elastic band on the first two. The engines didn't as much hum as cough, and on board, there was a strange smell. This was given away by the air hostesses wearing masks.

There were no sick bags, but plenty of buckets, and the reading literature was children's comics. Something about the First World War, which was about when this plane made its maiden flight.

The plane gets off the ground, to about ten feet, and I couldn't be sure if it was going to get any higher. You were not allowed to close the toilet door due to the fact it didn't have one. We now knew why the stewardesses were wearing masks. We eventually landed in Alicante, and trust me, there was one hell of a rush to get off that plane.

We went to arrivals to collect our luggage, which looked like it had been in a rugby scrum; collected the hire car; just about fitted all our luggage in; and off we went. By this time, it was dark, so finding the accommodation was not going to be easy. But find it we did, around midnight.

We arrived in Alicante on December 4. The weather was warm, and the villa we rented was a bit Gothic, akin to a crypt: dark, damp, nylon furniture, red kitchen, black curtains. The only thing missing was an open coffin. I have seen dungeons better dressed. The only good thing about it was that I could park the car outside. It had two bedrooms, one bathroom, and the bath was so small that if you had a shoe size of nine or bigger, you couldn't even stand in it. The main bedroom was upstairs, leading to a large solarium (sound like an estate agent, don't you think?).

Anyway, back to this Halloween villa. We slept upstairs. My wife, who usually goes to the toilet about five times a night, was frightened to go down the marble stairs in case she slipped. In Spain, there are no carpets. Everything is tiled; it's just too hot for carpets. In her wisdom, she decided to bring a bucket to bed. Peeing in a plastic bucket on a marble floor sounded like we were being invaded. The noise was horrendous, and it started all the dogs in the area barking, so you can imagine the fun everyone had trying to get to sleep. It was a topic of conversation. People were asking what that strange noise was that startled the dogs, making them bark every night.

Meg said to me, "Do you know?"

I said, "Yes, it's you."

We spent the next day unpacking and food shopping. Meg was brilliant, so organised. Being Christmastime, Meg was hoping we could access our stuff in storage, things like the Christmas tree, etc.

We soon moved into a more acceptable villa; then one day it rained, and did it rain! It was like a monsoon. There were ants coming from everywhere in the garden, like it was an ant convention, and these buggers had snorkels — that's how big they were, and that's how wet it was. There were millions of them. They could have marched on Poland, so we were once again looking for another place to rent.

I decided it was time I found myself a little office and decided to get into the rental market, finding places that people would be comfortable in. It could be good business, as, at this time, Spain was building like mad and people were buying to rent.

The new houses they were building, some of the workmanship was shocking, to say the least. As an example, the police found about fifteen Moroccans sleeping under this empty house that had just been built. When asked why they did not sleep inside the house instead of under it, they replied, "You surely are kidding! We helped build these houses. We're not staying. They are safe, but why take chances? We have small families to look after."

I also looked at the mortgage market, went around the banks to see if we could do business with them, and to my surprise, it was not a problem. There were no checks on me or my credentials. Amazing.

I made good friends with the director of one High Street bank and asked what the chances were of chasing mortgage debt that the bank may have. This was a problem they didn't care to admit, but it was there. When giving out mortgages, they just relied on two things: the valuation and the paperwork they were given. They couldn't check whether the paperwork was true or false. They were giving out mortgages with no proper checks, and losing their jobs in the process due to the increasing bad debt. This was an opening for me, as it was my type of work. Also, the one thing they couldn't find out was the type of credit history the clients had. Again, this is where I stepped in.

As a Master Broker, I had access then to Equifax Experian credit facilities. I had an account with these companies and could do what the Spanish banks couldn't. So, for a fee, which the banks invoiced the clients for, I said I could check out any problematic paperwork that was put in, could then tell them whether it was a good or bad application, to proceed or not.

Things really started to pick up. The bank's business was getting better, their debt less. Other banks heard of our work and every now and then gave us mortgages to check. From there, we went out to see the English clients who were having trouble servicing their borrowing with a view to restructure their payments and help get them on board again. When people are in debt, they believe only a miracle can help, but if you face it head-on, the banks are there to serve and will help whenever or wherever possible. It is in their interest to keep you in affordable debt. That may sound crazy, but it is a fact. So always face it; don't look the other way.

The banks wanted to see if we could sort out their arrears or find a way of restructuring their finances to suit both them and the clients. I mean, for banks then to repossess properties through the courts like today, it took on average over two years, sometimes three years. The backlog was so great, we even suggested they rent to their clients to save the properties from deteriorating, and maybe their fortunes would pick up, which would allow the mortgage to kick in before the court's decision to repossess, keeping the bank's property in good order and a client paying them the interest, that being the reason they lent in the first place. There is always an answer as long as you look for it — maybe not always to everyone's satisfaction, but it can reduce the heartache all this can cause and leave the banks in a better light, and more people-friendly.

All suggestions made just fell on deaf ears. They would not rent (they do now), would not give the mortgage holders a chance, so their properties fell into a state of disrepair, the people became homeless, and the money they were owed on the outstanding mortgage, which they were hoping to recoup on the sale, they couldn't get because of the condition of the properties. The price ended up as a giveaway or, worse, they auctioned the properties off and then tried to chase the clients for the balance of the arrears, which would be virtually impossible to get. They certainly were not forward-thinking.

I decided to open my first estate agency, and started to sell properties and finance. I had the repossessions from the bank as well as local properties. This was the best move we ever made, an absolute success. We employed a couple of staff with language skills and taught them selling skills, the way it should be done.

They were quick learners. This was reflected in their salaries at the end of the month. Meg and I bought an apartment or, as it was called, an upstairs bungalow; just a small place: two bedrooms, one bathroom, and a solarium with fantastic views and even better neighbours.

We invested in a car, only to find out Meg was the worst passenger in the world. She had a couple of lessons in England and thought she knew it all. She couldn't figure out why everyone in Spain drove on the wrong side of the road. In England, I took her out for a few lessons, but she was like a racing driver. In all fairness, she was a good little driver but had one major problem: she just couldn't overcome the roundabouts. She would go under them, over them, through them, but not around them.

I had a friend with a similar problem. Taking his motor bike test, he had a mental block about turning left. He just couldn't do it. He was fine learning, but test day just totally threw him.

Meg, she could be funny. I used to tell everyone she drove and I steered, which just about says it all.

As a hobby, I used to write poetry and short stories about the people I met: friends, clients through the business, and so on. One day, I decided I'd had enough of being told how to drive. She was the worst map-reader since I don't know when. I decided to quote a poem about her because I just couldn't think of any other way to get through. I called it "My Little Sat (Nag) Nav." It went like this:

I have a little sat nag; it sits here in my car.
A sat nag is a driver's friend; it tells you where you are.
I have a little sat nag; I've had it all my life.
It's better than them normal ones; my sat nag is my wife.
It gives me full instructions, especially how to drive.
It's thirty miles per hour here, it says, you're doing thirty-five.
It tells me when to stop and start and when to use the brake;
It even tells me it's never ever safe to overtake.
It tells me when a light is red and when it turns to green.
It seems to know instinctively when to intervene.
It lists the vehicles just in front and all those to the rear,
And taking this into account, it specifies each gear.
I am sure no other driver has so helpful a device,
For when we leave and lock the car, it still gives me advice.
It fills me up with counselling, each journey pretty fraught,
So why don't I exchange it and get a quieter sort?
Ah, well, you see, it cleans the house and sees I am properly fed.
It washes all my shirts and things and keeps me warm in bed.
I thought about the countryside and a horse and cart,
But may miss my little sat nag, who never snores or farts.
Despite all these disadvantages and my tendency to scoff,
I do wish once in a while I could turn the damn thing off.
I am considering two wheels, you know, the ones that sit up and beg.
Like a bit of a dog, really, no more trouble and strife,

No more my little sat nag I've had all my life.
I love you, sweetheart, but just let me drive.

She likes the poem, but her passenger skills are as bad as they've
ever been. I suppose every husband has this with wives that don't
drive. The TV series *Keeping Up Appearances* comes to mind. Mrs
Bucket, or Bouquet as she likes to be known, would love to take
control, and does to a certain degree, but what a grafter. Great
worker, puts me to shame.

Moving on. Business was good, and the staff was even better. We
had Nellie, a brilliant salesperson; Mark, who became my business
partner; and the lovely Bianca, who was just incredible.

We opened more shops and bought a big five-bedroom villa, had
a pool put in, and things were great. I decided I would like to try
my hand at opening a bar in Spain. Meg wasn't keen, but she always
trusted me. I told her that a bar was about personality and treating
customers how you want to be treated. I'd say it was one of the best
things we ever did, but she would say different. It was hard work,
but the people we met were just amazing. We ended up with some
wonderful friends we just love to bits.

I found out that the bar and restaurant called Harry's, where we
used to eat and drink on a regular basis, was becoming available. It
was magic, just what I wanted. Meg had a job looking after the
restaurant, and she was in her element, and the place was immacu-
late, gleaming.

The best bit about it all was the people we met. I could have gotten writer's cramp just listening to their stories, and boy, do they
have some! We had a group of regulars who loved to stand just
outside the toilets (these were close to the bar). It was a square area
and somewhere you wouldn't really want to stand; you're usually in
the way. People have, at times, to squeeze past you, and the smell
can be quite awful. Still, they loved that corner. They could see
everything that was going on, who was coming and going. I used

to call them the Muppets, so I made up a sign for them and called the corner the Muppioso corner. They loved it.

Something I found really amusing and nonsensical: They loved being insulted and ridiculed, as did most of our customers, and I could insult them all day long. It seemed like it was their fifteen minutes of fame just to come in and be insulted. It became a case where they were frightened to bandy words with me, but the characters were just wonderful. We had fantastic customers. They were no bother and would do anything to help. In fact, they used to run the bar. I used to just turn up. When we decided to paint and do a bit of refurbishment, I asked them to help. Believe it or not, they all turned up the following day with paintbrushes, toolboxes, ladders, and got stuck in. I supplied the coffee, beer, bacon sandwiches, and a free meal the following Thursday for them all to show our gratitude.

I used to write poems about them and the things they did, which they loved. Here are a couple. This was for the men and the corner where they all hung out. Each person who saw this masterpiece hanging up thought it was about them individually and not collectively.

I stopped them from swearing unless they were on their own in the toilet. We introduced a swear box, and it was a pound a word. It all went to charity. The bar had its name in the papers a few times for its charitable nature and its customers' donations, but did they suffer from flatulence. It was a challenge amongst them to be the worst, so I told them it had to stop, that the cockroaches were complaining.

I wrote the following:

A fart is a pleasant thing and
Gives the belly ease.
It warms the bed in winter
And suffocates the fleas.

A fart can be dry or wet,
A friend, your bum's very own pet.
A dry fart can be smelly
And tumble down the sheets,
Or hide under the pillow
To put you at your ease.
A wet fart can be sticky,
Not recommended here,
Running down from your bum,
Stinking of bad beer.
The love fart is the sweetest
When cuddling bum to bum,
Blowing kisses to each other
And keeping you both warm.
It's good to fart and air your view,
Like burping more or less,
As long as you don't follow through.
Shit, that leaves a mess.
So if you feel a rumble,
Remember where you are.
Not in bed, not at home,
In my fucking bar.

To be honest, I really don't think it had any effect. Everyone thought I was talking about them. You could hear them say to new people who came in or old friends who had never visited, "That's about me."

It was about this time someone suggested I write an agony column for the local magazine. Little did they know that the magazine, hearing about my antics at the bar, had actually approached me to do a fun column, so I suggested the agony angle, which they said would be different and unusual.

So, fame at last. My antics at the bar and the stories were attracting some attention from various quarters, so agony column it was, then. I called myself Uncle Donut. I had to make up my own questions and answers for the first issue, which went down quite well, but no one was writing in with any questions or thinking it was funny. Who is daft enough to have their life opened for ridicule in the local magazine? With this, people started collecting the issues to figure out who the idiots were with the problems. Of course, there were none. I did that for about six issues and decided to call it a day, but it was good fun making up the stories.

The names in the bar never matched the people themselves. They always made up names for each other. There was one guy there they called Humpty Dumpty. He was always saying to people, "Don't push me; don't push me." Another guy they called Nelson because he only had one arm (now how strange is that). There was Shaky Joe, who had Parkinson's; another, they called Lost. He suffered from Alzheimer's.

Ferrari John had a mobility scooter. Poor bugger was attached to a bottle of oxygen and carried his dog on the front of it — the scooter, that is. The dog got off every time John lit a cigarette and struck a match, oxygen still going. He used to light up like a Christmas tree, flames everywhere. Apart from the fact that he should not be smoking, he always forgot to switch the oxygen off when he used his lighter to light his fags. Strangely, the dog used to know what was going to happen, would step off the scooter, and was the only thing ever to take cover. They call them dumb animals; I am not so sure.

We had Trigger, who couldn't get anyone's name right, and Gary, whom I used to call Shrek because he was nearly the image of him. He got a bit upset about that. He said to me, "You telling everyone I look like Shrek?"

I said, "No, and you don't. His head's a different shape." With that response, he went away happy. A lovely guy, but you wouldn't want to meet him on a dark night somewhere. But if you did, you would want his autograph.

Finally, there was Flatulence Bill, who could fart for Europe, and the one who really gave me the idea for the poem.

I introduced a jamming session into the bar with the help of my mate Mick and a few other musicians. They used to play every Wednesday afternoon, from three to seven, and they were brilliant. It was an open mike session, which meant if you wanted to get up and sing or play an instrument, you could. It was sort of a poor man's karaoke. If you knew the words and were good, bad, or indifferent, you were welcome to get up. Some were really good; others could haunt a house. But it was all taken in good fun, and we were packed with all the nationalities you could think of. We organised live music two, sometimes three times a week, which included the jamming session, live music Fridays and Saturdays, and some excellent artists who could put to shame some of these talent shows, or better still, should be on them.

We were always busy. They (the customers) loved the music and loved to dance. It was new, you see. It livened the place up and the people, and one of the best things as a landlord is to see people going home laughing and enjoying themselves and, of course, coming back for more.

We never had any trouble. The people wouldn't allow it. We had problems, like the little gay guy (he was about four feet tall in his high heels) who used to come in a couple of times a week. We had nice settees for people to get comfy on, especially in the winter. It made the place appear that much more inviting, more homely, warmer. Well, Tim, we will call him, was sitting on one of our posh settees crying, and everyone was asking what the trouble was. He said he had lost his partner and that he had died in Ireland. Well, everyone was sympathetic and buying him brandies.

What they didn't realise was, his partner had died in Ireland, only three years earlier. At this point, he had drunk so much he started to wet himself on my settee, so I had Craig, another great friend, help him outside. I told him to bugger off and not to come back.

He looked at me and said, "Give us a hug."

I said, "You little bastard, if you were two feet taller, I would give you a black eye."

As I said: no trouble, nice people. He tried to take his clothes off at the top of the ramp. I stood there watching him, and when he finished, I turned the hose on him — dirty little man. Meg comes rushing out, feeling really sorry for him, not knowing what he has done, and tells me he is soaking wet and I should put him in the car and take him home.

I said, "What? Are you for real? Let the bugger walk."

But that was Meg. She'd help any poor soul, whatever they did.

The sad thing in all this is we had to give it up once the financial crash hit and was worldwide. People, especially the foreigners, just couldn't afford to come to Spain for their holidays anymore, even the ones who had holiday homes and apartments. No one was coming. Though we had great support from the locals, it wasn't enough. They didn't want us to sell, but I always said to Meg, the minute our estate agency had to subsidize the bar, it was time to call it a day.

We went on our first holiday in quite a while. We went to Hawaii for two weeks. We discussed the bar and the effect it was having not only on our relationship but on our funds as well, so we agreed it had to go. It was a shame, really. Everyone had worked so hard for us; even when we went on holiday, the customers (Stewart, mainly) ran the bar. It would be a sad day, telling everyone we had to put the bar up for sale. We didn't make a fortune out of it, but the friendships it created for us were priceless.

We had great staff in the bar, restaurants, and the kitchen, to whom I dedicate this part of my masterpiece. They were and still are good friends and even better people. We laughed and cried together, but at the end of the day, common sense had to prevail. No one can run at a loss. It went up for sale and was sold just under two years after we'd taken it on. We took it over from Harry Savage, a wonderful man with a wicked sense of humour, who sadly passed away and is talked about in glowing terms today.

I can say this, Harry, if you're looking down on me. You were a hard act to follow. Your daughter, Joanne, has it now. It's in good hands and doing a terrific job, but she always did, even when she worked for you and your lovely wife Jill, also sadly missed.

When we opened the bar, we knew two of the best people I have ever met in my life, Stewart and Arthur. Stewart was my best mate and the best man at my wedding, and was, we found out, a bit of a juggler. Meg and I got married in March. I thought that after seventeen years together, ten of those years engaged, she had passed the test and she was the one. So we decided on Gibraltar for our wedding. Being a British colony, it was so much easier than dealing with the red tape in mainland Spain. All our friends wanted to be there, and it was an honour for us and an unforgettable day. It was the day we found out about Stewart's juggling skills, and the masterful way he presented his best man speech.

From the wedding, we came home and prepared for our honeymoon with a cruise that took us to the French Riviera and the Italian Rivera. This was a wonderful present from Bianca and family. The star of the show that day, apart from my beautiful bride, was her stunning daughter, Yanis, our bridesmaid. So much so that everyone wanted their photograph taken with her.

The cruise was superb for me. I was a bit worried about Meg, as she gets seasick over a cup of tea. The ship moved off and I could see the panic in her eyes. That night, she didn't sleep. She woke me up at about three in the morning to tell me that the ship was rolling from side to side.

I said, "It isn't."

She said, "It is."

"Why on earth do you think that?"

She said, "I have fallen out of bed twice."

Our first stop, we docked in Marseilles. We spent the day there, and she spotted Notre Dame Cathedral. She said, "That's were Quasimodo lives."

I said, "No, that's the cathedral in Paris, also called Notre Dame."

She said, "There cannot be two."

I said, "Well, maybe this one is his summer residence."

The second night was different. She got a bit used to it, and she said, "It's true, you can't feel the ship moving."

Well, I didn't have the heart to tell her we were still in port, but the whole experience was simply fantastic. None more so than the visit to Rome, the Coliseum, and the Trevi Fountain.

Still married now and enjoying it, I was still a virgin after six months. I told my Irish mate and he said, "Don't worry; it's only six months. I have been with my wife for forty-five years and her legs have been together longer than the Rolling Stones."

I thought, *Thank God they're on their last tour.*

Another good friend we made at the bar, Arthur, was also funny. He and Stewart were sparring partners; talk about winding each other up! They loved everything about the war and war stories. Though he wasn't a serving soldier, even today Arthur takes his wife, Brenda, through Europe to visit the sights. I can see her now, with her tin hat on and gaiters around her ankles — one lovely lady. If you read this, *arf,* I really miss you, our talks, and BBQs at your villa, drinking my Scotch for days out. What a miss.

I fell ill with kidney failure and was close to death because of taking Ibufen. Stewart was like a brother and he still is. He was Meg's rock during the time I was in the hospital, 105 days, but it was Ibufen that nearly killed my kidneys. The great thing about kidneys is they repair themselves, and I now have 40 percent back. I was on dialysis fourteen hours a day, and in a real mess. Problems kept coming up, then my stomach blew up, and they gave me a 30 percent chance of pulling through. Prayers and well wishes from all my friends got me through, got all of us through those dark days. I really had all sorts of things done. They stapled me, stitched me, stapled me again. They were in and out of my body so many times they should have put a zipper in, but Stewart was there every day, sometimes twice a day, an absolute diamond. What a friend! Just incredible.

When he wasn't there, someone was. I felt so loved, so proud. I can never forget the doctors and nurses of Torrevieja Hospital who worked hard on me, the loving care of my beautiful wife, and also Bianca, who was sensational. They fought for me all the way. My mate Andy, who is now my pretend father-in-law (he walked Meg down the aisle), is the most loveable and generous man you could ever meet. I love him dearly, and his gorgeous wife, Linda. Sally and Anne and Bill; Pete, a great guy, were always there when I needed them. I'm not forgetting the lovely Brenda, Arthur's wife. Such a warm woman. There will be people I forgot to mention, but they all know how grateful I am of their support in what was a difficult time.

I was in and out of the hospital for nearly eighteen months, having various tests and more minor operations. I started my recovery from home, and after twelve weeks, I felt like I was ready to go back to work, but I wasn't really. I was still struggling to walk properly. When I first came out of the hospital after four months of just lying in bed, I had to learn to walk again, so it was a struggle. But we overcame that. They bought a Zimmer frame to help my progress, and I was surrounded by the best people anyone could wish for.

I was spending a few hours a day in the office and felt like I was on the road back, but looking in the mirror, I thought I was past my sell-by date. I honestly didn't expect to live too much longer, so I went about trying to put everything in place for Meg, expecting the inevitable. Still, I always felt positive, and life just got better. The nursing care and encouragement from everyone around me was just mind-blowing. It took another year to get the old legs working properly, and then I started back full time and joined the taxpayers.

I really feel good now and like to think I can handle everything that comes my way. Business? Well, it could be better, but we're paying our bills and salary, so we're better than most unfortunates. The housing market here in Spain died about seven years ago, and every year we tell ourselves the market has to change, and it will. I just hope I am around to enjoy it when it does. It's such a good investment here; the houses are cheap, the rental incomes are good, and you get far more for your money than you would by putting it in some savings or deposit account. The time at home did give me time for my favourite pastime, writing: poems, funny stories, I even started a novel.

So I wrote this book, and ardent readers will guess it's my first attempt, along with other numerous bits of literature, some funny, with lots of thoughts that may one day be published. For now, this is to be my legacy, to make a few people laugh and to say thank you. In sixty-five years, I have learned a hell of a lot. I feel that all of us ageing folks should give ourselves a pat on the back for getting this far in this mad world that has surely lost its way.

Now that I am older, here's what I have discovered: Worrying about the past can steal the future.

It's true what people say: It's hard to make a comeback when you've been nowhere. Growing up, some days you're top dog, some days you're the lamppost. Me? I am quite lucky. I started out with nothing and still have most of it. At the end of the day, also, it's easier to get older than wiser, but never forget, age is a gift.

CHAPTER 11

To Finish

I have been so lucky, and writing this as I get on in years makes me realize age is unimportant. Age is a gift, so I say this about my life and how I feel, and I ask everyone to study these next few words and maybe consider taking them on board.

Age is a gift.

I am probably, for the first time in my life, the person I wish to be. Not my body. I can sometimes despair over my body: the hidden wrinkles, baggy eyes, the paunch that I suck in that shouldn't really be there. My arse, now that's not bad. I am often taken aback by that ageing person who lives in my mirror. In all fairness to me, I don't agonise over those things for too long.

I would never trade my friends, my wonderful life, and my loving family for less grey hair or a flatter stomach. As I age, I become kinder to myself, less critical of myself. In a way, I have become my own friend.

I don't really tell myself off for eating those lovely chips, tasting that Magnum ice cream with the dark chocolate, not making my bed or closing the drawers, leaving my clothes where they shouldn't be. Who hasn't done those things? But I think I am entitled to a treat, to be a bit messy — to be, for want of a word, extravagant.

I have seen many good friends leave this world too soon or lie in a vegative state in a hospital before they understood the great freedom that comes with ageing. If I decide to dance with myself to the great music of the sixties and seventies or cry over a lost friend, a sad film, whose business is it? If I walk on the beach looking like less than a stud in a costume better suited to the jet set, whose business is it? For the jet set, they, too, will get old.

I know I am sometimes forgetful. There again, some of life is just as well forgotten. Eventually, I do remember the important things, happy or sad.

My heart has been broken over the years. How can a heart not be broken when you lose a loved one, when a child suffers, or even when a loved pet gets hit by a car or tortured by an insane human being? But broken hearts give us strength and understanding and compassion; a heart never broken will never know the joy of being imperfect.

I am blessed to have lived long enough to have my hair turn grey, and have my youthful outlook and laughter forever etched in the grooves on my face. So many have never laughed and have died before their hair turned grey.

I believe that as you get older it's easier to be positive. You care less about what other people think. I don't question myself anymore. I've earned the right to be wrong. Getting older, in a way, set me free, and I like the person I have become. I am not going to live forever, but while I am still here, I will not waste time on what could have been or worry about what will be.

I write this to myself as my friend lies in a hospital bed in intensive care, not knowing his lovely family. They, in turn, do not know if this lovely man will ever again know life as I do, cut down by the worries of the world, the stresses of giving his family the life he may never have had, by putting other people first.

I wish for a rainbow to keep them close, a cascade of love to keep them warm, and the pint he always promised me, which never arrived.

I write this to myself and people who, like me, are getting old. I

may never be understood, but I hope for the wisdom to understand. I have no desire to change or be changed, but just to live my
life in a thoughtful way and to help where I can, when I can, and
to be there when needed — to be an old friend.

I think it's important we find the time to make peace with our
past so as to not ruin our present. It's important to remember we
have no control over what happens to us, but only over what we do
when it does happen.

I know my age is my best friend. I know I cannot live forever,
but for today, and hope for tomorrow. Yesterday has gone, too late
for changes. Tomorrow can be a long time coming, which makes
today the most important day in our lives.

I would like to thank everybody for their help and support in
this, my legacy.

My thanks go to all the people I have mentioned and to all the
people I have forgotten to mention. You know who you are, and
you will never be forgotten.

Kindest regards,

Noel G.

Review Requested:
If you loved this book, would you please provide a review at
Amazon.com?

Lightning Source UK Ltd.
Milton Keynes UK
UKOW02f1543250716

279189UK00002B/148/P